June 2005

To Leah Rainbow
with warmest
good wishes
from MaryHannah

# WHEN THE SUN NEVER SET

# WHEN THE SUN NEVER SET

## A Family's Life in the British Empire

Alice M. Boase
with Mary Hannah (née Griffin)

Edited by
Margaret Knowlden (née Boase)

The Radcliffe Press

LONDON • NEW YORK

Published in 2005 by The Radcliffe Press
6 Salem Road, London W2 4BU

In the United States and in Canada
distributed by Palgrave Macmillan, a division of St Martin's Press
175 Fifth Avenue, New York NY 10010

ISBN 1 85043 943 5
EAN 978 1 85043 943 1

A full CIP record for this book is available from the British Library
A full CIP record for this book is available from the Library of Congress

Library of Congress Catalog card: available

Typeset in Sabon by Oxford Publishing Services, Oxford
Printed and bound in Great Britain by MPG Books Ltd, Bodmin

In loving memory:

of my late grandparents
AILEEN AND CHARLES GRIFFIN,

my late parents,
ALICE AND ARTHUR BOASE,

and my late uncle and aunt
JOHN BOWES AND EVA GRIFFIN

with my love and gratitude
for being part of their special family

*Margaret Knowlden* (née *Boase*)
editor

# Contents

# List of illustrations

# Acronyms and abbreviations

| | |
|---|---|
| BOAC | British Overseas Airways Corporation |
| CBE | Commander of the Order of the British Empire |
| CIA | Central Intelligence Agency |
| CMG | Companion of the Order of St Michael and St George |
| DOMS | Diploma of Ophthalmic Medicine and Surgery (later DO) |
| DSO | (Companion of the) Distinguished Service Order |
| FANY | First Aid Nursing Yeomanry |
| HMG | Her Majesty's Government |
| HMS | His Majesty's Ship |
| KC | King's Counsel |
| MBE | Member of the Order of the British Empire |
| NCO | non-commissioned officer |
| OBE | Officer of the Order of the British Empire |
| OSS | Office of Strategic Services |
| PK | lavatory |
| RAF | Royal Air Force |
| SS | steamship |
| UNIP | United National Independence Party |
| USSR | Union of Soviet Socialist Republics |
| VAD | Voluntary Aid Detachment |
| VD | venereal disease |
| VE | Victory in Europe |
| VJ | Victory over Japan |

# Glossary

| | |
|---|---|
| *anopheles* | malaria mosquito |
| *ayah* | nursemaid |
| *boma* | enclosure, corral (district headquarters in Northern Rhodesia/Zambia) |
| *box-wallah* | itinerant pedlar |
| *bwana* | master |
| *carozzi* | horse-drawn vehicle (Spanish) |
| *charpoy* | Indian wooden-framed string bed |
| *dhobi* | washerman |
| *doktari* | doctor |
| *double-terai* | double broad-brimmed felt hat |
| *dudu* | insect |
| *duka* | shop or group of shops |
| *fundi* | expert, craftsman |
| *hapana* | without |
| *jikoni* | kitchen, stove |
| *Kabaka* | King of Buganda |
| *kali sana* | very sharp or fierce |
| *kanzu* | full-length white cotton garment like a nightshirt |
| *katibwa* | prestige, kudos or amour propre, status |
| *Katikiro* | Prime Minister of Buganda |
| *khonde* | veranda |
| *kuni* | firewood |
| *kwacha* | independence/freedom/dawn |
| *Lukiko* | Buganda parliament |
| *machila* | pole-borne hammock carried by two or more people |
| *magezi* | common sense |
| *mama wangi* | my mother |

| | |
|---|---|
| *maridadi* | pretty or decorative |
| *matoki* | plantain, staple diet of the Baganda |
| *memsahib* | madam |
| *mpishi* | cook |
| *Mungu* | God |
| *mvuli* | mahogany |
| *mwengi* | banana spirit |
| *Nabagerika* | Queen of Buganda |
| *ngege* | delicious freshwater fish Tilapia esculenta |
| *ngoma* | beer party cum dance |
| *Omukama* | ruler of Toro district |
| *omulamazi* | chief justice |
| *omwanika* | treasurer |
| *pesi-pesi* | quickly or get a move on! |
| *piki-piki* | motorcycle or outboard motor |
| *pole-pole* | slowly or carefully |
| *saa kumi* | 10 p.m. African time, 4 p.m. Western time |
| *saa moja* | 1 a.m. African time, 7 a.m. Western time |
| *safari* | a journey |
| *shamba* | garden, cultivated plot, farm or the country |
| *shauri* | a bit of business or bother or, quite simply, a topic of conversation |
| *shenzi* | uncivilized, uncouth |
| *simu kuja* | telegram come |
| *tenga tenga* | head loads (Nyasaland) |
| *topi* | pith headgear |
| *toto* | child |
| *toto jikoni* | kitchen skivvy |
| *wangi* | my |
| *waragi* | nubian gin |

# British colonies lived in by three generations of the Griffin family

Charles and Aileen Griffin
| | |
|---|---|
| 1901–1914 | Nyasaland |
| 1914–1919 | Gibraltar |
| 1919–1921 | Antigua—The Leeward Islands |
| 1921–1932 | Uganda |

Arthur and Alice Boase
| | |
|---|---|
| 1929–1956 | Uganda |

John Bowes and Eva Griffin
| | |
|---|---|
| 1927–1935 | Uganda |
| 1936–1939 | The Bahamas |
| 1939–1946 | Palestine |
| 1947–1951 | Hong Kong |
| 1952–1956 | Uganda |
| 1957 | Northern Rhodesia |
| 1958–1962 | Uganda |
| 1962–1965 | Northern Rhodesia / Zambia |

Mary (née Griffin) and John Hannah
| | |
|---|---|
| 1958–1969 | Northern Rhodesia / Zambia |
| 1971–1973 | Turks and Caicos Islands |

# Editor's introduction

My mother, Alice Boase, privately published a small print-run of the first edition of *When the Sun Never Set* in about 1984. Having no distribution outlets, it mainly went to family and friends. I have been encouraged to believe that the colonial experiences of three generations of our family would be of interest to a wider readership and I am grateful to Dr Lester Crook of The Radcliffe Press for supporting this venture with a second edition.

Although it is popular today to decry colonialism, it was a way of life for many families and certainly one I feel very privileged to have enjoyed. Colonial ties and friendships have always had a special bonding quality. Whenever I meet up with former schoolmates and family friends, there is an instant recognition of shared experiences. Needing someone to write the Foreword for this book, it was heart-warming to know that I could call on our ex-Uganda family friend, Jim Dakin, now resident in Wellington, New Zealand, and I am most grateful for his generous input.

As an addendum to my mother's account, I have included my brother Peter's memories of an idyllic African childhood.

My mother originally wrote the second section for her brother, John Bowes Griffin. However, I have removed her version and instead included a more comprehensive account by his daughter, Mary Hannah (née Griffin), using notes her father had compiled; sadly he died before he could have them printed. His varied career is particularly interesting from an historical point of view. Mary's experience as the last of the 'colonials' is a fitting conclusion to one family's saga.

☼ ☼ ☼ ☼ ☼

Regretfully, I have to admit to two omissions from this chronicle. My paternal grandfather, William George Boase (born in 1865) was also a doctor and he too joined the colonial service. Posted to British Guiana towards the end of the nineteenth century, he married Marie Drysdale, who had been born and brought up in St Lucia, and the couple had five children. My father was the second of their four sons, and there was one daughter. Their story, had it been written, could have formed an interesting addition to this tapestry of colonial memories, but as far as I know this was never done. My father was a very private person, totally wrapped up in his career, for whom even letter-writing was a chore, let alone recording personal memories of life in a foreign land. Nor alas, did we think to ask. All we know is that, like the Griffins, the Boase family had to bow to the prevailing wisdom that the tropics were no place in which to bring up children. My father and his brothers were sent to England at an early age for education at Mount St Mary's, the Jesuit College near Sheffield. They did not see their parents throughout the war years, and holidays were either arranged by the school or spent with relatives — childless themselves and so all the more to be commended for taking on four young schoolboys.

The second omission is further reference to Kathleen, eldest daughter of Charles and Aileen Griffin and sister of Alice and Bowes, after her marriage to Charles Mullan. He took her to India where an account of her life as a civil servant's wife might have added an extra fascinating dimension to the Griffin family saga. Disappointingly, this was not to be.

Finally I must thank my cousin, Mary Hannah, for her encouraging involvement in this book. She has been a tower of strength with suggestions and painstaking proofreading, as well as meticulous research, photographic searches and personal accounts. Our joint project is also a symbol of the generational bonds that have grown so affectionately since the newly-wed Charles Griffin and Aileen Fanning took those first intrepid steps into the unknown in 1901. We both feel privileged to be part of their now very extended family.

Margaret Knowlden (née Boase)
Sydney, Australia

# Foreword

I t is a privilege to be asked to contribute a foreword to
the second edition of Alice Boase's lively book about her
experiences in several British colonial territories, especially in the Uganda Protectorate. This book is almost unique
in that it gives valuable insights into the life of the wives and
families of the colonial officers whose achievements have in
general already been recorded in many historical works.

As an administrative officer in Uganda in the 1940s and
early 1950s, I came to know Alice and her medical officer
husband through my first wife Eleanor who, as a nursing
sister, had had a close association with them in the government outstation of Fort Portal. Throughout our years in
Uganda, my wife and I kept in touch with the Boases. Before
and after each of our four children was born, and I was in
the army or in an upcountry station, Eleanor stayed with
them in Kampala and received valuable comfort and advice
from Alice. Such was Alice's helpful attitude towards friends
and many others despite her own heavy family commitments.

By 1947 Alice and her husband were bringing up a family
of ten happy children, the older ones spending nine months
a year at boarding school in Kenya. Ably assisted by a
reliable staff, she was able to devote time to charitable work
and public affairs. She was already active in cultural circles
as a cello player and as an actress in amateur dramatics.
Following her husband's involvement in local public affairs,
she became a member of the Kampala Municipal Council
and joined the Uganda Council of Women, an influential
multiracial body. These activities eventually led to her being

nominated as a member of the Legislative Council of Uganda — one of the first two women to serve on that body of which leading Africans had only recently become members for the first time. As a member of this council she took part in many of the discussions that led up to the independence of Uganda.

Retired with her husband in 1956 (before they embarked on a new career with the St John Eye Hospital in Jerusalem), she continued to be active in family and other affairs, but found time to write two books, one of mainly family interest and the other, this one, of much wider interest. It gives a lively account not only of her own experiences but also of those of her father and brother, both of whom worked for many years in several colonies as well as in Uganda. It also includes an account by her brother's daughter, Mary, who through her husband followed the family tradition. The result is a very perceptive portrayal of the lives of colonial officials and their families in the last years of the Empire. She writes sympathetically of the poignancy of family separations when wives or children had to leave for reasons of health or education. She does not refrain from describing the frustration or boredom of young women without children who stayed on while their husbands or fathers were intensely preoccupied with absorbing work in which women could rarely take part.

There is a vividness in her descriptions of local African life. She remembers that 'on wet Sunday mornings it looked as if large green caterpillars were on the move, as churchgoers made their way uphill in their hundreds under "umbrellas" of banana leaves'. The depiction of such scenes enlivens the narrative and recaptures the peaceful atmosphere of most of the colonial past.

Jim Dakin
Commissioner of Community Development, Uganda
(retired 1953)
Wellington, New Zealand

# Griffin Family Tree

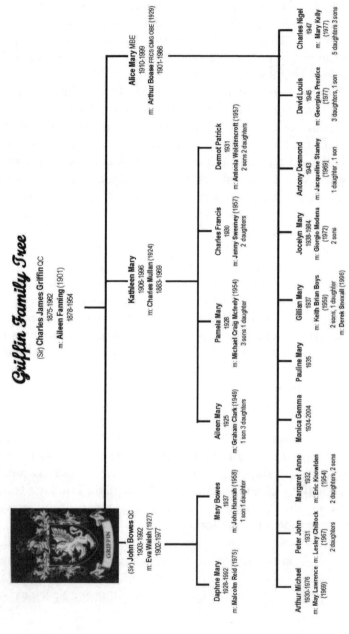

(Sir) **Charles James Griffin** QC
1875-1962
m: **Aileen Fanning** (1901)
1878-1954

**Kathleen Mary**
1906-1996
m: **Charles Mullan** (1924)
1883-1969

**Alice Mary** MBE
1910-1999
m: **Arthur Boase** FRCS CMG OBE (1929)
1901-1996

(Sir) **John Bowes** QC
1903-1992
m: **Eva Walsh** (1927)
1902-1977

**Daphne Mary**
1928-1992
m: Malcolm Reid (1975)

**Peter John**
1931
m: Lesley Chittock (1967)
2 daughters

**Mary Bowes**
1937
m: John Hannah (1958)
1 son 1 daughter

**Arthur Michael**
1930-1976
m: May Lawrence (1969)

**Margaret Anne**
1932
m: Eric Knowlden (1954)
2 daughters, 2 sons

**Monica Gemma**
1934-2004

**Aileen Mary**
1925
m: Graham Clark (1949)
1 son 3 daughters

**Pauline Mary**
1935

**Pamela Mary**
1928
m: Michael Craig McFeely (1954)
3 sons 1 daughter

**Gillian Mary**
1937
m: Keith Brian Boys (1959)
2 sons, 1 daughter
m: Derek Snoxall (1996)

**Charles Francis**
1930
m: Jenny Sweeney (1957)
2 daughters

**Jocelyn Mary**
1938-1984
m: Giorgio Modena (1972)
2 sons

**Dermot Patrick**
1931
m: Antonia Wolstencroft (1957)
2 sons 2 daughters

**Antony Desmond**
1943
m: Jacqueline Stanley (1969)
1 daughter , 1 son

**David Louis**
1945
m: Georgina Prentice (1977)
3 daughters, 1 son

**Charles Nigel**
1947
m: Mary Kelly (1977)
5 daughters 3 sons

GRIFFIN

# 1

# Charles and Aileen Griffin

To the best of my two-year-old knowledge, I had never set eyes on the woman whose attentions I was determined to resist. But, young though I was, I sensed in her appearance a threat to the world as I knew it and, more especially, to its presiding deity, my nanny, in whose eyes I could do no wrong.

It is hoped there are few people whose most vivid early memory is of repudiating their own mother, but that this was my experience provides an illustration – albeit a somewhat extreme one – of the sort of situation that bedevilled family life in the British colonial service. There were to be few changes for the better up to the 1940s. Indeed, it was not until the post-Second World War years, when colonialism itself was on the way out, that the picture was dramatically altered by improvements in health and living conditions and in the means of travel and communication.

It so happened that my birth in Dublin in 1910, when my parents were on leave from Nyasaland (now Malawi), practically coincided with the celebration of my brother's seventh birthday. This was an important milestone in the lives of all colonial children for it was generally deemed that, after that age had been attained, no European child should – or, quite literally, could – continue to live in the tropics.

Our parents had resigned themselves to leaving John Bowes, the eldest of their three children, in Ireland.

1

1. Aileen Griffin with Alice as an infant, Kathleen aged 4 and John Bowes aged 7, Dublin 1910.

Certainly, in view of the very real health hazards and total lack of education facilities in Nyasaland, they had no alternative.

They had arranged that he should live with our paternal grandmother in Dublin while attending day school. But it was felt that he would need more care and attention than the old lady could be expected to give him. So they arrived at the decision that I – the new baby – should also be left behind so that they could feel justified in installing a nanny to look after us both.

Sometimes in later childhood, when feeling 'unloved and misunderstood', I would work myself up to believing that I had been abandoned in infancy. But I am sure my mother must have hated to turn her back on a small baby and it just seemed the best thing to do in generally unsatisfactory circumstances.

Well, blood may be thicker than water but I had no sense of affinity with my parents when we were reunited two years later and, throughout their leave, I steadfastly rebuffed every attempt at reconciliation. Even so, I was aware that I was fighting a losing battle and it was with no real surprise that I eventually found myself being prised from Nanny's arms and setting off – wailing dismally – with my parents and older sister on the long journey to Central Africa.

As for my brother, now being left behind for the second time, it cannot be said that he was enjoying his translation to the Emerald Isle, adapting to both a new home and schoolwork. Life in our grandmother's house and later at boarding school contrasted sadly with the free and easy existence he had enjoyed in Nyasaland. In the early days, particularly, he must have been acutely miserable and his only diversion seems to have been provided by the weekly appearance of an organ-grinder and his little, blue-coated monkey, though the excruciating renderings of 'Danny Boy' and 'When Irish Eyes are Smiling' were not calculated to cheer.

It is impossible to estimate the damage done to family relationships by the separation of parents and young children, for they never really caught up with each other again. A few years make a big difference to a child's development. So reunions were never easy and, just when a familiar footing was being established, it was time to part once more. It could be said that my brother and other children in similar circumstances were the 'displaced persons' of that era.

Meanwhile my protests continued unabated on board ship. My poor mother must have been at her wit's end when an attack of measles proved to be a blessing in disguise. In the midst of my spotty misery, she became the source of all solace and comfort and memories of Nanny gradually faded into the background.

I expect this illness must have occupied most of the voyage for otherwise no memories of it remain. Nor to my regret do I recall any details of the journey up from the coast of Portuguese East Africa to Nyasaland, now Malawi, which was partly by riverboat and partly by rail. This was destined to be my last experience of river travel for, by the time we left Nyasaland two years later, we were able to cover the whole distance by rail.

## British Central Africa/Nyasaland: 1901–14

My father, Charles Griffin, must have been fairly typical of the early recruits to the colonial service. Although some may have joined because of a sense of adventure, by far the greatest number did so because they were impecunious young men who were finding it hard to make their way in their home country. They were glad of a job that offered a measure of security, steady if unspectacular prospects and a pension after 20 years in the service.

A quarter of a century was to pass before the majority of these young men were required to have any specific training or even a university degree. Although the legal and medical intakes were exceptions in this respect, most of them were newcomers to their profession and had to gain their

4

experience the hard way. Well into the 1930s, the director of public works in Uganda had no engineering qualifications whatsoever.

My father was the youngest of a family of five and had been hardly more than an infant when his father died, leaving his widow in fairly straitened circumstances. Charles proved to be a clever boy and, although his real interest lay in English literature, he followed the family tradition by studying law and was called to the Bar. It was no easy matter for a young barrister without private means to establish himself in those days. So, before long, he was weighing up the pros and cons of a congenial lectureship in New Zealand and a less congenial but better paid magistracy in British Central Africa. At that point he met his future wife and decided, for better or worse, on the magistracy.

Africa was still a very dark and mysterious continent at the turn of the twentieth century and information about it was not easy to come by. Even the 'great man' who interviewed my father at the Colonial Office seemed rather in the dark. When asked how one travelled to British Central Africa, he replied – after much humming and hawing – 'You take a boat to Aden and go overland from there.' Presumably, a more reliable source of information must have been found, for in September 1901 my newly married future parents, duly equipped with all tropical necessities in the way of solar topis, spine pads, cholera belts and mosquito boots, were on their way.

My parents were neither an adventurous couple nor remarkable for their physical courage, but they must at least have been brave in spirit to take this vast step into the unknown. Their voyage, via Suez in a tiny German ship, was a lengthy adventure in itself – and no more comfortable than adventures usually are – and their arrival in Portuguese East Africa only marked the end of the first stage of their journey. Even the actual disembarkation was something of

2. 'Basket' used to embark or disembark passengers at Chinde.

an adventure: ships had to anchor outside the shallow harbour and passengers were packed into a large wicker contraption – just like an enormous clothes basket – in which they were winched from ship to barge.

Having, metaphorically at least, come down to earth with a bump, they then had to travel up the Zambesi, and later by its tributary the Shire River, in a succession of boats of decreasing draught. Such amenities as refrigeration and air-conditioning had not, of course, even been thought of in those days and, although their clothes were of 'tropical' weight, they were formal and constricting in the current fashion and did nothing to mitigate the heat and general discomfort of their situation. The only diversion that seems to have relieved the tedium of those hot, mosquito-ridden days was provided by the antics of crocodiles as they basked and slithered in the shallows.

When the river was no longer navigable, another form of

transportation awaited the travellers. The final stage of the journey to Blantyre was done in hammocks, known as *machila*s, which were slung on poles and carried on the shoulders of porters. The anti-colonialists' worst fears will be borne out by this picture of tyranny and servitude. But I believe the bearers were quite oblivious of the ignominy of their task and jogged cheerfully along, keeping up a rhythmic chant in which, no doubt, there were many ribald references to their human burdens. I cannot discover what distance was involved in this part of the journey but my brother, whose last experience of it was in 1910 when he was nearly seven years old, can recall no camping *en route*. So I assume it must have been accomplished in the course of a day; nonetheless, it was tough going, with a steep climb from the river valley up to the Shire highlands.

Meanwhile, vast quantities of luggage also complicated this odyssey, for all the personal and household needs for the coming tour of two to three years had to be provided. There were packing cases and crates, tin uniform cases, which rapidly acquired an extremely battered appearance, cabin trunks of compressed cane and stout leather suitcases. Each item was supposed to represent a head load of 30–40 lbs maximum, so it has always been a mystery to me how so many upright pianos – an essential piece of furniture in every gentleman's household – managed not only to reach their destination but also did so in remarkably good order. Perhaps they, too, were provided with *machila*s.

My parents seem to have weathered their travels remarkably well; and also remarkable was the ease with which they adapted to living conditions that were completely different from any they had previously experienced. Admittedly, life in European countries still lacked many of the refinements we now take for granted. But in Nyasaland and other African colonies then – and for many years to come – such basic conveniences as piped water and waterborne sanitation were unheard of.

3. Charles and Aileen Griffin at home, teatime, Blantyre 1902.
Transported Edwardian décor achieved by determination!

The young couple's first house was an uninspiring little brick box with calico ceilings over which rats squealed and scampered by day and by night. Accommodation comprised three rooms in a row, flanked fore and aft by verandas that provided, respectively, additional living and utility areas.

Off the bedroom were a couple of small rooms designated 'dressing' and 'bath' rooms. The latter's equipment included a washstand with the usual utensils, a zinc tub to be filled on demand by the cook's assistant, and a commode to be used only on occasions of dire need. More general use was made of an earth closet in a hut in a remote corner of the garden, the supposedly inconspicuous appearance of which was frequently given away by a rampaging tropical creeper, which had been planted in the first place for its hoped for concealing properties. The water supply, which depended on rain running off the corrugated iron roof into tanks at the corners of the

4. Charles and Aileen Griffin, Blantyre. One hopes that there were other, larger and stronger men to pull a second rickshaw as Charles Griffin was no stripling even then, 1902.

bungalow, was never really adequate and the gardeners (which were referred to then as garden boys) had frequently to set off with the ubiquitous paraffin tin on their heads to the nearest spring. Lighting was by oil lamps and the cook functioned with the aid of a wood-burning stove in a smoky little hut at the far side of the back compound.

The normal amount of luggage was augmented in my parents' case by a great number of wedding presents covering every sort of domestic requirement, including silver, linen and crockery. I cannot imagine how they and their belongings managed to fit into that little bungalow, but their servants must have been delighted at such a lavish display, for they were great snobs and liked their employers to put on a good show.

Even this unimpressive establishment was staffed in the manner of the day – and of many colonial days to come –

by a small regiment of servants, all of whom were referred to as 'boys'. There would have been at least two houseboys, a *dhobi* (laundry-man), a cook and his underling and a few garden-cum-rickshaw boys. The combined efforts of the five house servants about equalled those of a couple of European domestics and they needed a great deal more supervision. Servants' wages were reckoned in shillings rather than pounds and they provided their own food, which was mostly grown in their smallholdings. My parents became very attached to their African servants – indeed my mother never really resigned herself to those of a lighter complexion – and their shortcomings and peccadilloes were regarded much as are those of a mischievous but endearing child.

In fact my father was not much better off than his domestic staff, for, on a salary of £300 a year, he was expected to keep up a decent household and sartorial standards and had, moreover, to contribute to his mother's support.

On the credit side it must be said that he had free housing – such as it was – with basic furniture, and leave on full pay every few years. Best of all, there was no income tax to pay. Also on the credit side was the fact that they could live mainly and very cheaply on local produce. Imported goods were expensive and in no great variety, though an occasional tin of stewed beef, known as 'Machonicie's Rations', provided a welcome change from the usual tough meat and stringy chickens. Most people kept a few hens, for, although eggs cost only one shilling (five pence) per 100, they were minute in size, very dubious in quality and quite unfit for the breakfast table. To this day, one can tell an ex-colonial woman by the care she takes to break each egg separately into a cup, while her abhorrence of a dripping tap reflects those early anxieties about the water supply.

My mother had a very real gift for homemaking and she was delighted to have a free hand with her little house, away from parental advice and interference. Photographs show that, with the aid of a few draperies and knick-knacks, she achieved a remarkable example of Victoriana in Central Africa and she and my father were certainly very well pleased with the results of her efforts.

They were to spend 13 years in Nyasaland and seem to have led a near idyllic existence, marred only by the prevalence of malaria and dysentery. Parts of Nyasaland were literally 'white men's graves' and even in Blantyre an attack of 'fever' every month or so was something every adult took for granted. Where children were concerned there could be no such complacency, for in their case infection could be extremely serious and even fatal. Quinine was then, and for many years to come, the only known cure and it was quite impossible to administer it orally to children. Anti-malarial measures, other than the use of mosquito nets, were virtually unknown, so I have always regarded the fact that my brother, sister and I escaped infection in childhood as no small achievement on our mother's part. Even so, in the existing sanitary conditions, she could not entirely circumvent another tropical hazard; I can remember severe tummy upsets, which must, I imagine, have been due to bacillary dysentery, for there was mention of blood and I could sense her anxiety.

I doubt if my father's official duties were at all taxing. Indeed government itself was on simple lines, which were all that was necessary in relation to people who were feeling the first breath of civilization. Nonetheless, law and order were maintained and this in itself must have made a nice change for the local people – though perhaps life may have seemed a bit dull without the excitement of inter-tribal raids and skirmishes, which had played such a large part in their earlier history.

Social life for the small European community was pleasantly simple and non-competitive because the handful of officials, the managers of a few agencies and the personnel of the Scottish Mission were all in a similar boat financially. The ladies of the Scottish Mission were notable housewives and it was from them that many an African cook learnt his trade. My mother also benefited from their kindly instruction and some of their well-tried recipes have become part of our family tradition – though with certain modifications such as four eggs in place of a dozen of the Nyasaland variety in a Christmas cake.

My brother's birth in April 1903 was fortunately an uncomplicated affair, for my mother and the young doctor who attended her were about equally new to the job. Shortly after the birth the family set off on home leave by the complicated route (in reverse) already described. This was a truly formidable undertaking with a small baby and, from all accounts, it was one that he only narrowly survived.

I think it must have been when they next went on leave in 1906, when my sister Kathleen was born, that they took an African nurse-boy with them. The mind boggles at the thought of this very unsophisticated young man being accommodated in my grandmother's household. Not surprisingly, his pram-pushing outings caused great excitement among Dublin girls to whom, at that time, he was a complete novelty.

Some time before I joined the Blantyre household, my parents had been given better housing, which, in retrospect, seemed to have comprised quite spacious accommodation though still, of course, lacking even the most rudimentary mod cons. I was only four when we left Nyasaland so my memories tend to be of isolated scenes and events. But it was at this stage that I learnt to dread the spectacular thunderstorms, which are a feature of Africa's rainy seasons, and even 40 years later I still hated those simultaneous flashes and crashes that seemed intent on our destruction.

One of my most vivid memories is of the excruciating boredom of cricketing afternoons when I was supposed to

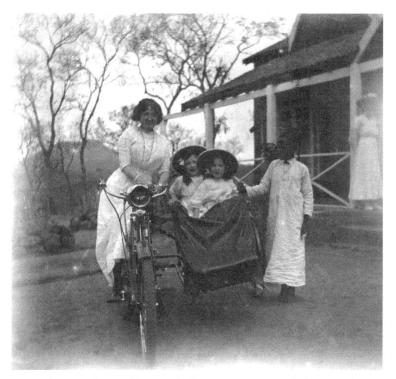

5. Aileen Griffin, Kathleen and Alice trying out one of Blantyre's first motorbikes with sidecar. Speed limit was 10 m.p.h. *circa* 1913.

amuse myself quietly without disturbing the almost church-like solemnity that such occasions then demanded. To my mind, their only redeeming feature was the tea break when the ladies vied with each other in producing a delectable array of cakes.

Rickshaws provided our normal transport but, on at least one occasion, I can remember sitting in breathless excitement at my mother's feet in the sidecar of a motorcycle, which must have been one of the first to be seen in the country. Another innovation was my parents' HMV gramophone, complete with an enormous horn out of which I always hoped a fox terrier would emerge.

I have, too, a hazy recollection of a holiday up on Mlanje Plateau – chiefly memorable because a leopard made off with the chicken intended for our next day's lunch. I remember little of the actual journey to Mlanje but I believe we went as far as possible by *machila*, then small children were carried, while older ones and adults walked. But women – naturally clad in ankle-length garments – were hoisted up the steeper slopes by means of a towel or sheet looped around their bodies from waist to thigh. My mother told me that the ascent was punctuated by the sound of corks popping out of bottles that contained fermenting yeast for making bread.

Government officials' salaries were subject to regular increments, but they must have been on a very small scale because when, in 1914, my father was offered the post of attorney-general in Gibraltar, this not only meant substantial promotion but a big jump in salary – to £800 a year.

Although my parents were very pleased about this improvement in their prospects, they were naturally very sad to be leaving Nyasaland where they had been so happy and had so many friends. A final Nyasaland memory comes to me of my mother shedding tears among the packing-cases – a procedure which was to be repeated on another occasion as the exigencies of my father's career brought further upheavals and moves to the unknown.

This time we travelled to the coast by rail. But it seems to have left no impression on my mind, except I vividly remember finding myself swaying in that clothesbasket over the deck of the *Llanstephan Castle*. We were to have sailed via Suez and disembarked at Gibraltar. But when the declaration of war was followed almost immediately by the information that a German raider was lying in wait for us on the northern route, we had to turn tail and make all possible speed around the Cape and thence direct for England. All this was, of course, quite beyond my ken and I was very disappointed to learn that we would not be travelling by the Red Sea, which I had confidently expected to live up to its name.

This sudden involvement in the perils of war must have caused great anxiety to the crew and to the adult passengers and, although at the age of four I was immune from such considerations, I can remember the eeriness of companion-ways lit only by candles standing in buckets. Other memories of this voyage are of coming up on deck with my sister early in the mornings for the express purpose of watching the pyjama-clad Aga Khan – grandfather of the present holder of the title – performing physical jerks, and of the inevitable children's fancy-dress party for which I was dressed as a cracker in very prickly crêpe paper.

Almost coinciding with the outbreak of war, and temporarily at least of closer significance to my parents, was the astonishing news of a native uprising in Nyasaland. The instigator, whose name was Chilembwe, had been educated in the USA and returned home burning with nationalist-cum-religious fervour.

He was 'agin' all authority and was particularly averse to the Scottish Mission, whose tenets he regarded, rightly or wrongly, as militating against tribal traditions and customs. The movement had little support and was quickly contained, but not before at least one European had been murdered and the others very badly frightened indeed – almost as much by the total unexpectedness of the episode as by the violence it engendered.

In the manner of the *Mikado*, Chilembwe had drawn up a list of those who were to be exterminated and of how the deed was to be done. Some, including my father, were merely to be killed any old how, while others, including the victim already mentioned, were to be beheaded and the heads placed – as his was – on the altar of the Scottish Mission church. The wife of the murdered man had a narrow escape because a faithful servant rushed her off into the bush and kept her in hiding until the trouble had subsided.

Our altered travelling arrangements were not entirely unwelcome to my parents as it gave them the opportunity to spend a few weeks in Ireland with Bowes, by then aged 11. If it had not been for the transfer to Gibraltar with its good climate and adequate schooling, Kathleen would also have had to be left behind at this stage, for already she had exceeded the tropical school age limit by one year.

## Nyasaland: a wider view by Mary Hannah

Alice and her older brother and sister were all under ten years of age when they left Nyasaland. Their childhood memories give little impression of living conditions prevailing in that part of Africa between 1901 and 1914. Fortunately, records are available that can augment Alice's own lively descriptions and give an idea of the practical, everyday problems and their solutions that her parents experienced.

Alice recorded how new arrivals landed from their ships at Chinde. This small settlement was a good 338 miles from Blantyre. It was in Portuguese territory, but there was a British Central Africa agent to smooth their transit through local controls. There were customs duties of 5 per cent of their value on all clothing and personal possessions. River dues of one shilling per hundredweight were also payable.

They arrived at the end of October, the hottest and most unpleasant time of the year before the rains came. The few buildings at Chinde were built precariously around the mouth of the Zambezi in an area where the course of the river frequently altered, and it was a particularly unhealthy spot with mud flats and swampy areas.

Chinde boasted a small wooden hotel with a corrugated iron roof and verandas outside the rooms on each of its two floors. Travellers stayed there if the arrival of their ships failed to coincide with the departure of one of the small river paddle steamers that provided the means of transport for the next stage of the long and tedious journey, a journey that could last for up to two weeks and that headed at first north-westwards along the Zambezi River.

There were several of these steamers, operated by the African Lakes Company and by an enterprising individual called Eugene Sharrer. In theory the boats departed regularly and frequently, but the 'Africa factor' could and did affect the timetable. In November the river was at its lowest, which made navigation more difficult.

The boats were far from luxurious. They had one or two upper decks with a few cabins for European passengers and a small deck where meals were served. The river valley and swampy banks were perfect breeding grounds for mosquitoes, which were a problem despite attempts to screen the open deck and cabins with wire gauze, while cockroaches thrived in the crannies and came out at night to add to the discomfort.

The tight, formal clothing fashionable at that time, which must have been extremely hot, was in fact a useful protection against being bitten, and there was every need to take care; it was not unusual for new arrivals in Blantyre to fall ill with fever within days of the river journey. Keeping cool and fresh was impossible on board, for the only washroom was extremely primitive, with a jug or two of water in a tin basin providing for what could only be perfunctory washing.

Because it was too dangerous to attempt navigation in the dark, the boats were tied up to the river bank at dusk, and there were recognized halts near woodpiles kept to supply fuel for the paddle steamers. It was sometimes possible to go onto the river bank and cool down in a hip bath, filled with murky river water, in a hut with a mud floor and a grass or animal skin flap over the doorway for privacy. Back on board it was difficult to sleep in the stuffy little cabins without even the small breeze felt when the boat was in motion.

Progress was slow at the best of times and, as the scenery was monotonous, the novelty soon wore off. There were occasional villages and birds like fish eagles, some antelope, crocodiles and hippos; the latter had been known to attack steamers occasionally. If the boat ran aground crewmen had to brave these hazards when they jumped overboard and pushed and poled the vessel until it floated again, to the accompaniment of much shouting and excitement. The daily tedium was broken by unappetizing meals, nearly always of chicken. The cookhouse was on a barge tied alongside the main steamer as a fire precaution, and the baskets full of clucking birds gradually emptied as the days went by. Food was hauled up from the barge below and brought to the passengers on their patch of deck.

At the point where they left the Zambezi for its tributary, the Shire River, the direction changed to almost due north and at Chiromo, 250 miles from Chinde, it was necessary to change to smaller boats, with even less comfortable facilities, as food was now all tinned or of the picnic variety and was eaten on the river bank. The Shire valley was stifling and the swamps stretched for miles, with reeds and mangroves. At a place called Katunga's, 310 miles from Chinde, the river ceased to be navigable and at last the journey was on land. There was another basic hotel at Katunga's, and we know the Griffins reached this point on 11 November 1901. In terms of distance they were now only 28 miles from Blantyre, but there was an extremely steep path to be tackled on the way, called in those days the Cholo escarpment, and now marked on maps as Thyolo. The Shire valley is about 300 feet above sea level and Blantyre stands at 3500 feet.

Alice has described the single pole and hammock type of

*machila*, but a photograph taken of her mother at Katunga's shows that in fact she was about to set off in a more sophisticated model, carried on two poles, with a canopy to shelter her from the sun. Passengers would semi recline on a litter propped up by cushions, and a coat or rugs would be needed early in the morning when they set off or when it rained.

Each *machila* had a team of 16 men, who took turns carrying the load and who were paid three shillings a month, plus their rations. Going uphill the *machila* would be turned so that the passenger's head went first, whereas on the flat their feet would face the front; in either case it provided a swaying, lurching sensation and going up the narrow track on the escarpment must have been alarming with a steep drop to one side. If all went well four miles an hour were covered, so it was possible to reach Blantyre in one very long and tiring day if an early start were made, which was desirable anyway to take advantage of the lower temperatures. It was, however, possible to break the journey at a rest house run by the African Lakes Company halfway between Katunga's and Blantyre.

Meanwhile, also in the procession were carriers known as *tenga tenga*, who conveyed the luggage on their heads. Anything larger or bulkier would eventually arrive in Blantyre on one of the few carts pulled by oxen. Later, some traction engines were imported and there were a few carts or carriages drawn by mules and horses, but tsetse fly meant that these were difficult to keep. Apart from the use of private *machila*s within Blantyre, local movement around the township was also achieved by means of rickshaws, an idea introduced by Consul Hawes, one of the early consular staff who had previously worked in Japan. The teams pulling these, or those carrying *machila*s, were dressed in matching uniforms.

It was not until the railway was built that transport of people and goods became easier. Finance for the railway was raised partly in London and partly by the same Eugene Sharrer who had been involved in the river steamers, but it was only in 1908 that the first train reached Blantyre, an event that Bowes Griffin remembered witnessing at the age of five. The governor and his wife were passengers, and the front of the engine was draped with a flag, while along each side tender young banana trees had been tied upright as decorations. There were a few bicycles in Blantyre early on, while the first motorcycle was imported by Sir Alfred Sharpe in 1903, and the first car in 1908. A speed limit of ten miles an hour was imposed in the township.

By 1901, when the Griffins arrived there, Blantyre had been established for 25 years and, though officially a 'township' with a council and such signs of civilization as a valuation roll and rates, it was still only an area of roughly five miles across, composed of a number of widely spaced pioneering settlements separated by tracks and undeveloped bush. The earliest group of buildings had been constructed by Church of Scotland missionaries who began their work in 1876, to the north of the Mudi stream. Two years later the Moir brothers, with financial backing from others in Glasgow, arrived and set up what was to become the African Lakes Company to the south of the river at Mandala. The wall and towers they built to protect their compound from possible attacks by the Ngoni were known as the fort. There were several buildings to house staff and a rest house to cater for people coming from Mandala stations further upcountry on visits to the head office in Blantyre. Further north, at Kubula Hill, Eugene Sharrer and Frank Ryall were among other early pioneers; the former seems to have had a finger in every pie related to early commercial and transport development, while the latter set himself up as a builder and started a furniture workshop (and much later became the proprietor of Ryall's Hotel). There were a few other small traders and a Mr Keiller had started a hotel that was patronized by planters and other travellers.

One wide street, Victoria Avenue, ran south from Kubula Hill to the government buildings. These were in a cleared area known as Boma Square, which was in front of the *boma* and which housed the legal offices and courtroom built in 1900. Trees had been planted along both sides of the avenue, on which there was also a post office. Mail to Europe took at least six weeks and there was a telegraph service via Salisbury and Cape Town. Banking facilities became available when the Standard Bank of South Africa opened a branch in 1896.

There were a few bungalows for government officials in Victoria Avenue and one of these, opposite the *boma*, was the Griffins' first home, and the birthplace in 1903 of their son John Bowes. Each house had a veranda, known locally as a *khonde*, and keeping house had its own challenges.

All servants were men – even a 'nurse man' for the baby in due course – and they needed strict supervision in order to maintain hygiene when water, insects and disease were constant threats. All the water, apart from that collected off the roof when it rained, had to be fetched from the river, which kept one servant occupied much of the time. Water from hipbaths or washing crockery and clothes would be recycled for optimistic attempts to grow vegetables and fruit.

Apart from the food grown in the garden, produce could be bought at the local market when available and another servant, known as 'the fowl boy', would be away sometimes for days at a time scouring the villages for chickens at a few pence each, and eggs at a shilling per hundred. Milk and butter were mostly tinned because it was difficult to keep cattle. Very occasionally it was possible to buy goat, sheep or bullock meat.

Employers were told to send their servants with orders to the butcher's premises the night before animals were due to be slaughtered, for this was done early in the day to avoid the heat, and the gory cuts of meat were immediately carried back to be cooked the same day. Payment for produce bought from the local people was still often made in the form of salt, calico and beads, and the traders imported brightly patterned 'native goods' to appeal to their taste.

As far as possible the Griffins lived on local produce, with the occasional treat or necessity bought from traders if and when available. The *Central African Planter*, a newspaper started in 1895, carried advertisements announcing the arrival of consignments of goods from Europe and South Africa. Surprisingly, items sold included champagne – hardly an essential – but also other wines, spirits, soda water and cigars and tobacco.

The hardware on offer included spare parts for bicycles and lamps, building materials, camping equipment such as folding furniture, guns and ammunition, boots and shoes. Some toiletries and patent medicines could be obtained, as well as men's clothing, cufflinks and collar studs; little provision was made for women's tastes or needs, but some cloth was imported, and in 1911 a Singer sewing machine was advertised for £5. When an advertisement for an unusual item appeared, like the one that proclaimed 'BACON! BACON! BACON!' it was necessary to react quickly, for each consignment was small and latecomers would be disappointed. Indeed, for anything coming from outside the country, it was a case of feast or famine. There was a steady demand for second-hand household items sold by auction when people left the country or died.

In 1895 the European population of Blantyre was recorded as 133, of whom 12 were women. There is no figure available for 1901, but two new faces must have been welcome. Even though there were so few expatriates, life was still formal and few concessions were made since maintaining standards was considered good for morale. Evening dress was worn and anything by way of a special occasion was celebrated with as much ceremony and effort as could be contrived. There are menus showing dinners with several courses, all in French and beautifully printed at the local print shop, as well as dance programmes and lists of events for the annual sports week and agricultural shows.

Photographs show the courtroom bedecked with flags and banners, palm trees in pots around the piano and stage, and rows of non-matching chairs, borrowed from all the households to provide seating for the concerts, amateur theatricals and other functions held there before 1903, when the Queen Victoria Memorial Hall was built and the court-room was thenceforward reserved for its real purpose.

The Blantyre sports ground, which had a pavilion, was also the setting for games, races and matches, after which dances would be held, despite the men far outnumbering the women and the cement floor being hard on the feet. At that time the Central Africa Regiment, with British officers, Sikh NCOs and the first local African recruits, had a band and would play music as it paraded on special occasions on the Boma Square or sports ground. When the regiment went to the west coast to take part in the Ashanti operations, there was a formal welcome on its return.

As well as public occasions, there were picnics, and tennis and croquet matches, which were of more interest to the ladies than cricket and athletics. Recipes were exchanged at female gatherings, including a lethal sounding concoction to cure constipation. Sewing parties were organized to produce works for sales and the costumes for theatrical productions and fancy dress parties. The children were not forgotten; a photograph of 14 of them shows the boys mostly in white sailor suits surrounding a cosily outfitted Father Christmas.

Strenuous efforts were clearly made to enliven what could have been a lonely and monotonous existence for the few women. The men had the interest of their work, although this was at a level that could often be contained within a few hours each day.

By 1913 Charles Griffin had completed his work on the laws of Nyasaland. Legal officials undertook both judicial and administrative work, which was allocated to specific dates and days of the week. The *Gazette* would put out public notices saying that the court would sit for general business on the first Tuesday of every month ('unless otherwise ordered'). Matters that could be 'summarily disposed of' were to be heard by summons in the judge's chambers on days fixed by him. Petitions and motions were to be settled on Fridays. Members of the public were warned that when court business was the day's work conveyancing matters had to wait. The judges also went on circuit. Probate administration occupied all too much time: there were 14 expatriate deaths in one year, a measure of the need to take extreme care over health precautions.

At the headquarters in Rome where the archives of the White Fathers (missionaries of Africa) are kept, records have been found of the negotiations that took place before the foundation of a Roman Catholic mission eight miles from Lilongwe, at Likuni.

The Church of Scotland missions were well established in British Central Africa and in 1901 the *Nyasaland Times* carried a headline 'There is no place for the Papists'. In that pre-ecumenical and pioneering era, the denominations were understandably territorial (in the most Christian way).

It was sheer coincidence that both the legal officials at that time in control of land registration and granting permission for a new mission were Irish Catholics, Judge Nunan and Attorney General Charles Griffin. The two officials gave the permission needed for the new foundation, but were scrupulous over the formalities involved in the face of the objections raised. Likuni, however, was a very long way from Blantyre, so it was possible to avoid trespassing on each other's areas of influence. For many years the fine church at the Blantyre mission was the only ecclesiastical building in Blantyre. It was a prominent landmark that had been designed and built, with Gothic and Norman arches, under the supervision of the Reverend David Scott and his

6. Church of Scotland Mission occasion, Blantyre. Clothing made no concession to the African heat *circa* 1901.

brother in 1888. The bricks for the building were made on site and local labour, which the Scottish Mission had trained in building and carpentry, was used. With its predecessor a much more modest structure, it towered over any other building in the town.

The Church of Scotland Mission had also provided the only medical care available in the early years. It was as a result of the loss of one of the mission doctors that moves were started in 1895 to establish a public hospital. Several wards in separate bungalows were built on a slight incline to the south of the *boma* area, known as Sunnyside. Money was raised for this and for the salary of a doctor independent of the mission. The new hospital was in operation at the beginning of the century and would have been among the first group of buildings the Griffins passed at the end of their *machila* journey on that day in November 1901.

Judge Nunan, whose remarkable photographs give a

clear idea of life in Blantyre in those early days, was Charles Griffin's immediate superior until 1903. He resigned to take on family responsibilities at home in Ireland and the resulting promotion meant the Griffins moved to a much bigger and better house, which was called 'Nyambadwe' and which Alice has described. Her brother Bowes was delighted and amused to find the house still standing, and still inhabited by a judge, when he revisited Blantyre in 1957. In many respects the conditions the first generation of the family experienced were not really very different from those Alice knew in Uganda in the 1920s, or that the Hannahs – the third generation – saw in Northern Rhodesia in the 1950s. The biggest improvements to the quality of life of course were the motorcar, paraffin fridges and faster postal communications.

## On the Rock: 1914–19

The four years we spent in Gibraltar seem, in memory at least, like a very pleasant slice of eternity. I was too young to be affected by the anxieties that beset my elders as the war news went from bad to worse. Life for me seemed to be compounded of parties and picnics, pleasantly interspersed by schooling with the kind Loreto nuns on Europa Hill.

My parents came to like living on the Rock very much indeed, but to begin with a lot of adjustments had to be made. Life suddenly took on a very urban aspect after the rural simplicity of Nyasaland and I think my father's work was a good deal more demanding. Inevitably, the cost of living was considerably higher and, despite a rise in salary, they found it difficult to make ends meet.

Fortunately, two opportunities arose for my father to augment his income. The first of these came about because, as Attorney-General, he was, in official terms, the 'Proper

Officer of the Crown Prize' whose job it was to 'seek condemnation of prize [captured] ships and cargoes'; he was entitled to a fee in respect of each case; although I do not know what they amounted to, I can remember my father saying that the sum made all the difference between debt and solvency.

The other source of income was his editorship, in his spare time, of the *Gibraltar Chronicle*, which was also the official gazette, and for this he was paid £100. The proofs used to arrive at our house at noon and after lunch my father would pencil in his comments and corrections, which must have constituted a poser for his staff because his writing was quite illegible.

All in all, I should think that his annual income at that time must have been about £1000 and to my recollection we lived very comfortably, with three or four Spanish or Gibraltarian servants to wait on us – it would never have occurred to anyone that we could possibly have managed on fewer. My mother found these servants far more difficult to cope with than the African variety. For one thing they were rarely stayers. Matrimony, often to British servicemen, tended to carry off the more attractive ones and our only faithful retainer over the years was an amiable but simple soul employed as a nursery-housemaid, for whom there were no marriage prospects.

We lived midway between the Anglican cathedral and the back premises of Government House, in a large house in Secretary's Lane that had previously been used as a police station and still had bars on some of the downstairs windows. The house was built around a patio and had three storeys plus a lookout on the roof. It actually had electricity and waterborne sanitation and we also had piped water, though the fresh sort was in very short supply and we used to bath in seawater.

In all, our new home presented far more of a challenge to our mother's homemaking talents than those simple African bungalows had done, but her flair did not desert her. With my father's encouragement – for he too enjoyed visiting salerooms and picking up attractive furniture and other household goods (some of which, I might add, are in the family to this day) – she soon had the place looking very nice indeed. Even as a small child I was aware of comparing it favourably with the homes of some of our friends.

Gibraltar was full of service personnel, many of whom seemed to regard themselves as belonging to a higher form of life than the rest of us. Inevitably, some of this rubbed off on their children and when we forgathered in the Alameda Gardens with our nursemaids and played among the cannons that had seen service in the Crimea, there was great one-upmanship about the importance of our respective fathers. I was glad that mine, as Attorney-General, had the right sound at any rate.

The summers in Gibraltar are long and hot and we used to swim twice a day. In the mornings we would go to the Ragged Staff pool, which was only a few minutes' walk from our house, but in the afternoons we would take a picnic tea and go further afield. During our first summer we spent many happy afternoons at Catalan Bay where there was a little fishing village; later we transferred our allegiance to nearby Sandy Bay, which, with its glistening sands, myriad of shells and exciting rock pools, was a veritable child's paradise. Above the road that led to these bays the sloping rock face was thickly encrusted with sand, which, we were told, was regularly deposited by wind blowing across the straits from Morocco. Twice while we were in Gibraltar the sand slipped down onto the village and practically engulfed the little houses. I visited the scene with my mother who was involved in some charitable effort on behalf of the villagers and I saw people climbing in and out of the upper part of their windows. Thereafter I was never entirely happy when we were on that road and always kept an anxious eye on those sandy slopes.

Cars were still a rarity and we usually got about on foot, though with a *carozzi* to take Kathleen and me up Europa Hill to the Loreto school and my mother on the round of visits that were so much part of social life at that time. Later we acquired a trap with an extremely temperamental pony and a series of equally temperamental 'boys' to look after them. Occasionally, we were lent a car and chauffeur and it was thrilling to bowl along at what seemed like a breakneck pace through the Spanish countryside. Unfortunately, we had first to drive through the frontier town of La Linea, for whatever it is like now it was then a most squalid little place and the car had to straddle the cobbled streets that sloped steeply down to a central drain into which every sort of refuse and effluent found its way.

My brother was able to join us for the summer holidays in 1915, travelling with some other boys by the overland route, but when the time came for their return the war situation was so grave that their parents could not risk the hazards of the journey. So he and his contemporaries remained in Gibraltar where they had a most enjoyable time and were not unduly inconvenienced by such schooling as was improvised to meet the emergency.

Shopping with my mother was something I enjoyed very much. The main street was a lively, interesting place, with several shops selling oriental goods and restaurants that specialized in an enormous pancake carried around in flat trays on the waiters' heads, which I longed – unavailingly – to sample. Off the main street was the so-called Jews' Market where a discerning eye could sometimes pick out useful and even valuable articles among a miscellaneous assortment of junk.

Our visits to the ordinary market were chiefly in search of eggs, which seemed to be an expensive and unreliable commodity; although our Moorish egg man used to scrutinize each egg carefully against the light, this seemed to be no guarantee of its freshness. This gentleman came over regularly with his wares from Tangier and, when he heard that we were going there on holiday, he insisted we should visit his home. This we did in due course and in his absence the wives in his harem entertained us to sticky sweetmeats and a liberal sprinkling of rose-water.

This holiday has left me with vivid memories, though it started with a terrifyingly rough crossing of the straits in a boat I am sure would no longer be allowed to put to sea. It was in Tangier that I had my first experience of Eastern-style markets and bazaars, which were later to hold such a fascination for me; I loved the narrow lanes, colourful stalls and spicy smells. Every afternoon we would join the crowd that gathered to hear the storyteller's latest episode in a seemingly endless serial. Although we could not understand a word he said, we felt caught up in the breathless excitement of his spellbound audience.

No one can live in Gibraltar for any length of time without encountering the famous apes whose survival on the Rock has been superstitiously linked with that of the British themselves. In general, they were harmless creatures, but they could get up to mischievous pranks and were especially attracted to the washing-lines on the flat roofs. On one occasion they made off with a couple of frocks that happened to be our Sunday best and, when they were recovered several bananas later, their Sunday status had gone beyond recall.

Gun practice was a regular and necessary feature of life in wartime Gibraltar, for the possibility of an enemy attack was very real. But only on one occasion were those guns brought seriously into action when it was thought that a German submarine had entered the harbour. It occurred with dramatic timing on the stroke of midnight on New Year's Eve 1917 when, in accordance with custom, the governor had just stepped out onto a balcony to address the populace. All hell was let loose and everyone was very scared and shaken, but it was in fact an inconclusive affair because there was never definite proof of the submarine's presence. Not quite everyone was disturbed, however, for to my bitter chagrin I had slept soundly throughout the din.

At the beginning of the war, sovereigns had been withdrawn from circulation and it was, indeed, illegal to possess any. It is a measure of the anxieties of those days that my father – normally the most law-abiding of men – kept a secret hoard of these coins so as to be able to provide for his family if the worst happened and he had to send us to Spain for safety. He reckoned, no doubt correctly, that gold would always be acceptable whereas British Treasury notes might not be worth the paper on which they were printed. After the war those sovereigns were doled out to us as birthday and Christmas presents; they were worth just £1 sterling.

Although I had known little about the war, I remember the easing of tension as things began – at last – to go our way. I well remember the excitement of Armistice Day and then the terrible anticlimax of the mass funeral of the men of HMS *Britannia*, which was torpedoed within a few hours of the signing. Most members of the crew were saved, but between 40 and 50 lost their lives. Standing with my mother by the roadside it seemed as if the procession of gun carriages was never ending.

Before either of these events, however, Gibraltar had been in the grip of the Spanish flu epidemic, which took a heavy toll on the population. My father seemed to be perpetually attending funerals, while my mother – the only victim in our household – lay desperately ill. Our servants decamped and everything devolved on my sister's 12-year-old shoulders.

Almost miraculously, our mother recovered, the epidemic waned and life resumed its normal course, though I doubt if my brother thought so when he found himself packed off back to boarding school in Ireland. For all of us, in fact, those Gibraltar days were drawing to a close, for our father had accepted the chief justiceship of the Leeward Islands. This offer had posed a dilemma for our parents: on the one hand the West Indies had a reputation for being a bit of a dead end career wise, but on the other hand to refuse a promotion did not make for popularity at the Colonial Office. So, willy-nilly, the offer was accepted. I am sure that these misgivings were a contributory cause of those tears among the packing cases as our mother prepared for our move to the western hemisphere.

## The Leeward Islands: 1919–21

When we set out for Antigua, the capital of the Leeward Islands, in March 1919, Kathleen and I were nearly thirteen and nine-years-old respectively and should, by rights, have joined the displaced persons in Ireland. But we were reprieved because our parents had been assured of suitable schooling and a reasonably healthy climate in the West Indies.

Our many travels must have constituted a sore trial for my poor mother, for I was an appalling sailor and had been known to succumb to the mere smell of paint and grease as we climbed a gangway. Our voyage to Antigua was no exception, though on the first part of the journey, which took us to Nova Scotia, some Canadian soldiers inadvertently proved that mind could triumph over matter when they allowed me to join them in a couple of games of Crown and Anchor.

Nova Scotia gave us our first experience of glacial weather and also, paradoxically, of what seemed to us to be excessive central heating, for in the hotel in which we spent a few days the windows had been sealed up for the duration of the winter.

It was quite a relief to board our ship for the onward journey, though it seemed to be a perilously small one – and I missed those Canadian soldiers!

With most colonial postings, a house went with the job and – rightly or wrongly – my father always maintained that he had been assured at the Colonial Office that one awaited him in Antigua. So it was quite a shock to discover on arrival at St John's, Antigua's capital, that no house had been provided and that it was to prove almost impossible to find a suitable one to rent.

A very weary round ensued, for, with the collapse of the sugar trade, the island had reached the nadir of its fortunes and on every side poverty stared us in the face. There was hardly a single house that was not in dire need of painting and repairs, and the few available for renting were in the last stages of dilapidation. Trailing along in the wake of our parents, I could sense their deepening depression as one impossible proposition succeeded another. Things were really getting desperate. Our father was on the verge of arranging that my sister and I should return to Ireland with our mother when one of the few well-to-do planters offered us the use of his 'town house'.

My parents thankfully accepted this offer and I am sure were far too glad to have a roof over our heads – and a sound one at that – to quibble over the furniture and décor, which could hardly have been to their taste. My chief recollection is of very scratchy red plush, which did nothing to ease the irritation of prickly heat on my arms and legs.

As far as 'conveniences' were concerned, we were almost back to Nyasaland standards. There must have been piped water because I can remember standing under a shower in a zinc bath, which was built into a corner of the bathroom, but oil-lamps replaced the electricity we had grown accustomed to in Gibraltar and 'sanitation' was an earth closet in the garden.

The thing I remember most about Antigua in those early days is the piercing night-time orchestra of the insects, which almost bore a hole through one's head with its intensity. However, we were told that it was a reassuring sound because if the insects kept quiet it meant that a hurricane was on the way. Very soon, of course, we got so used to the noise that it often took a conscious effort – and a few anxious moments – to get on the wavelength at all.

Our servants were black and mostly women, but the best of them shared a dual ambition to get to the USA or Canada as quickly as possible and to have their hair straightened when they did so. Fortunately, we acquired a rather splendid butler who rejoiced in the name of Henry Leopold Armstrong. He was the soul of dignity, as befitted an elder of one of the many Christian sects and, as he moved majestically about his tasks, his *embonpoint* wore a hole through a succession of aprons. Fortunately for us he was a strict teetotaller, for he frequently had to deputize for our cook when she came reeling home from the local rum shop.

Although the climate was regarded as healthy, we found it very humid and enervating and all the white people had a thoroughly washed-out appearance. Of course this may have been due, in part at least, to the quality of the food, which in those pre-refrigeration days left much to be desired. Apart from the inevitable tough meat and stringy chickens, we relied heavily on guinea fowl, which were reared dom-estically, and on land crabs, which played a large part in the local diet – every backyard contained a barrel in which a number of the creatures were kept so that they could be effectively purged of their impurities on a diet of chillies before meeting their fate. Vegetables were extremely insipid and fruit was disappointing, especially the black pineapple, Antigua's emblem, to which my father had been greatly looking forward but that proved merely to be an unripe pineapple. My only mouth-watering memory is of Arm-strong's coconut ice cream, which invariably graced our Sunday lunch table, but ice cream of any sort was a great treat in those days.

It was in the garden of our new home that I had my first fascinated glimpse of a humming-bird, hovering like a quivering jewel over its thimble-sized nest.

To the rear of the house there was an enclosed yard and through the gate every Saturday morning came a strange procession, which went from house to house collecting alms by right of custom. Cheerful to a man (and woman), they hobbled along on an assortment of peg legs, crutches and grotesquely swollen limbs, for all were victims of filaria, so aptly known as elephantiasis. This disease was by no means confined to the black population. There were some unfortunate women among our parents' acquaintances who could not avail themselves of the shorter postwar fashions; men were similarly afflicted, but at least trousers offered a fair chance of concealment and shorts were still unheard of.

No time was lost in packing Kathleen and me off to the girls' high school. Here my father had certainly been well informed, for its ramshackle buildings quite belied the high standard of teaching that the formidable headmistress, Miss Branch, aided by her sister and various younger relatives, meted out. The male members of this same remarkable family staffed the boys' grammar school and the people of Antigua and the neighbouring islands were fortunate indeed to have their children's education in such capable hands.

I believe both schools received government grants that precluded racial segregation. But although black and white children mingled quite amicably in the classroom, the integration went no further. Yet it is a little black girl called Beryl whom I remember more clearly than any of my lighter-skinned classmates. She was always immaculately dressed in starched cotton frocks and her wiry hair was coaxed into tiny plaits that stood out on either side of her head, tied with strips of matching material. Once – greatly daring – I invited her to see my rabbits in their hutches underneath our veranda and, although that was the full extent of our social interaction, she certainly left a vivid impression.

35

Many years were to pass before 'integration' came to play such an important part in our life and in our vocabulary. Most of our friends were, like ourselves, children of civil servants, although I believe the majority were island-born and locally appointed, while others lived on estates owned or managed by their fathers; we were also friendly with a few families of Portuguese descent.

The only comment I remember my father making about his work was when he expressed shocked surprise at finding that the local population regarded perjury lightly, if at all. They in turn were astonished at his attitude to what was to them a perfectly normal procedure, and I doubt if the subsequent investigations and prosecutions on the part of the police and the attorney general had any long-term effect on what was obviously a time-honoured custom.

On the first occasion my father came home to lunch after a morning in court he was accompanied by a dog with rather vague Labrador connections, which, he said, had joined him 'on the bench'. As no one thought to explain this term to me, it conjured up, in all seriousness, a vision of this large animal and my 18-stone father seated side by side in mutual discomfort on a plank of wood. Apparently Rufus had developed the habit of attending court when he belonged to the previous chief justice and he certainly assumed that he went with the job because he took up residence with us as a matter of course – and continued to sit on the bench.

The Court of Appeal met twice a year, each time on a different island, and we greatly envied our father his trips to Trinidad and Barbados, both of which sounded much more exciting than Antigua. Unfortunately, it was not possible for us to accompany him because of the expense involved, though on occasion we got as far as Montserrat, which was, quite literally, next door.

The courthouse in St John's, though of no great architectural merit, was a reasonably substantial building. But the shops were dingy little shacks with very basic stock in trade that offered no temptation to go on a spending spree. Our spheres of activity were within easy walking distance so, although there were more cars than there had been in Gibraltar, we did not own one. Sometimes our mother would hire a car in order to visit friends on an estate and it was a treat to accompany her and widen our horizons, although the countryside was not really very attractive. We had hoped for good picnicking and swimming facilities, but the beaches proved disappointingly remote and jellyfish were a frequent hazard. St John's harbour was unsuitable for bathing for obvious reasons, so we relied chiefly on parties the school organized when we were taken across the harbour by longboat to Fort James, where there was a fine beach and enjoyable swimming – jellyfish permitting.

When we had been only a few months in the house that had been loaned to us, another one became available. I remember it as being brighter and pleasanter in every way, though its name, 'The Manse', was hardly appropriate for a Catholic family and the owner struck a depressing note when showing us around by assuring my parents that a window placed at an angle of the stairs was 'so convenient for turning a coffin'.

One of the advantages of this house – and a rare one in that hurricane area – was that it had a very large veranda and, constituting an even greater advantage in my eyes, two swings hung beneath it. This veranda was so spacious that on at least one occasion it was used for an informal dance with music provided by the local steel band, which was much in demand for all entertainment. I am nearly certain that some of our Saturday visitors were among the players for there were crutches and peg legs sticking out onto the floor and, when my mother apologized for tripping over one of these, the owner assured her, with a broad grin, that it 'didn't hurt none'.

The band did not have a very large repertoire and it

could be relied on to fall back on what was, I suppose, a calypso, though I doubt if such a glamorous name was applied to it then; both words and music were simple and repetitive, and the former went like this:

> Bam-Bam Sukie – Sukie dead!
> Bam-Bam Sukie – Sukie dead!
> Sukie never dead but she sell last night!
> Sukie never dead but she sell last night!

This theme was repeated over and over again and at first we were mystified until friends enlightened us. It seems that many years previously one of the planters had owned a cow to which his wife had become very attached. She extracted from him a promise that the animal would never be killed or sold, so she was very distressed when he informed her one day that it had died. Still, nothing could be done about that and she was resigning herself to the loss when a herdsman spilt the beans. 'Sukie never dead but she sell last night'! History does not relate what she said to him (or vice versa), but I am sure neither of them expected the tale of their mutual discomfiture to echo down the years long after they had passed beyond all care.

My parents seemed to have had a gift for making friends and settling down in new surroundings and I think they even found a certain refreshing simplicity in the Antiguan social life compared with that of Gibraltar. Very soon indeed my father realized that, on a salary of £1200, he was vastly better off than all officials except the governor. There had been no allowances made to offset the increased cost of living, for prices had risen steeply during the war and many people were experiencing real hardship. He thereupon took the unusual step of conducting a one-man commission of inquiry and then presented the governor with a report, which first annoyed him considerably and then shocked him into taking action. It seems incredible that he should have been unaware of the state of affairs, but he was big enough to be grateful to my father for bringing it to his notice and very soon there were many delighted recipients of backdated increments. Over forty years later I was to learn that my father's action was still remembered with warm appreciation.

My father had an inordinate fear of the tropical sun and solar topis were compulsory for all members of his household. These struck an unfamiliar note in Antigua where lighter headgear was considered quite adequate. I was once dreadfully embarrassed when a coal-black mammy shrieked across the road to a friend: 'Will you look at the judge's darter in a bowler 'at!'

Antigua's one outstanding feature is English Harbour, where Nelson was based as senior captain between 1777 and 1786. Some friends took us there in their car and, although my historical knowledge was sketchy in the extreme, the haunting atmosphere of this beautiful harbour with its deserted jetty and sail lofts fascinated me. On a bluff overlooking the water was a derelict house once occupied by the Duke of Clarence and there was a sense of trespass as we picnicked in the shade of its crumbling walls. Long afterwards I learnt that British seamen had dreaded this seemingly benign anchorage because the prevalence of yellow fever had given it an evil reputation for sickness and death. It was no wonder that the atmosphere was haunting.

The black population was a cheerful lot though without, one would think, very much to be cheerful about, although Carnival time was the great occasion for jollifications. I suppose it was a pre-Lenten affair but it probably owed as much or more to African memories as to the more recently acquired Christianity. Most of the goings-on were quite beyond my ken, but the torchlight procession filled me with spine-chilling excitement because it was more than a little alarming to have a ghost's lantern-illuminated face appearing at my bedroom window.

Undoubtedly the most exciting event in Antigua's social calendar while we were there was the visit of the Prince of Wales (later King Edward VIII and eventually Duke of Windsor) who came to the island at the end of a world tour on board HMS *Renown*. Our house on the main street was well placed to see him drive through the town in an open car and our maid added a red necklace to her blue-and-white uniform and hung out of an upper window in the hope that he would notice her patriotic colour scheme. We high school girls, resplendent in our white American-style sailor suits and pork-pie hats, duly paraded for the Prince's inspection and sang the inevitable 'God Bless the Prince of Wales'. We thought the young prince looked terribly tired and our parents, who were among the official reception committee, told us that his right hand had been so over-enthusiastically pumped in the Antipodes that he was obliged to shake hands with the left one.

Although my parents had settled down happily enough in Antigua, my father had taken every opportunity to remind his overlords at the Colonial Office that he was anxious for a transfer as soon as possible. One day my sister and I came home from school to find him and our mother in a state of pleasurable excitement. It seemed that there had been an offer of the chief justiceship of Uganda. Soon we were all poring over the atlas and identifying that particular pink blob among the many that littered the globe in those days. This was promotion in a big way and our parents' only regret was that this time Kathleen and I would have to be left at school in Ireland. Secretly we were attracted by the novelty of this prospect, but I expect we put on a polite show of regret at being unable to accompany our parents to their new posting.

We had spent only 20 months in Antigua and my parents were sad to leave the many friends they had made there, some of whom my mother kept in touch with to the end of her life. However, they looked forward with a sense of homecoming to their return to Africa – their first love – and this time there were no tears among the packing cases.

## At home: 1921–26

Our parents were considered fortunate in having relatives who were willing to look after their children during the holidays; others had to make use of so-called 'homes from home', which rarely lived up to their name. My mother told a story, which she certainly believed to be true, about two little boys from Nyasaland left in one of these establishments who, when friends of their parents visited them unexpectedly, were found to be officiating as pages.

It cannot have been easy for grandparents to have the even tenor of their days disrupted by a youthful influx during the holidays, probably for several years at a stretch. Nor was it easy for the children to fit into those elderly households. Although we heard nothing about the generation gap in those days, it was there nonetheless and there were stresses and strains for all concerned. Some households coped remarkably well, usually when there was an unmarried son or daughter who acted as a buffer between old and young; others were less successful. But even when the situation was actually unhappy, no one forgot the all-important axiom that parents in far-flung outposts of empire must on no account be worried by complaints. Indeed, it is hard to know what they could have done, with letters taking a month or more on the way and no possibility of a flying visit in the modern manner.

Even in the best circumstances none of us colonial children really felt 'at home' and most of us grew up with idealized memories of our extreme youth and a longing to return to them at the first possible moment. Perhaps it was out of this nostalgia that the colonial service became, as in my brother's case, a 'tradition', for he certainly never wavered in his determination to go back to Africa. His daughter, Mary, memorably records his career later in this book.

My parents' leave in 1923 was highlighted first by my father's knighthood, which appeared in the Birthday Honours, and then by my sister's engagement – an event that surprised no one but me and led to her exchanging our colonial scene for the Indian Civil Service. The next leave came in 1926 when I was 16 and it was with considerable pleasure that I learnt that I was to go to a finishing school in Switzerland before joining my parents in Uganda.

I had spent over five years at Loreto Abbey, Rathfarnham, County Dublin where, in the manner of the day, my education had been fairly sketchy though probably not much worse than that of most of my contemporaries. So it was for the likes of us that finishing schools flourished on the continent during the 1920s and 1930s. They certainly provided a pleasant interlude between the schoolroom and the grown-up world. But, apart from smoothing rough edges and imparting a moderate fluency in a foreign language, they did nothing to prepare one for life with a capital L.

Very few middle-class parents then thought in terms of any sort of training or higher education for their daughters; my father would have regarded any suggestion of the sort as an insulting reflection on his ability to provide for us. It seemed to be assumed that my sister and I would make satisfactory marriages – and the sooner the better – but not even with this aim in view did it occur to any of us that a little instruction in the domestic arts might not come amiss. To tell the truth, servants were such an accepted feature of life, at home and abroad, that none of us imagined ever being without them.

More by good luck than good management, things were to work out as my father had so confidently expected, with my sister and I marrying both early and suitably. But I am appalled to recall with what ignorance I at least embarked on the responsibilities of married life and feel my husband had much to put up with. When my sister married in 1924 and I married in 1929, my father insisted that both sons-in-law should take out life insurance to the value of £1000. He thereby felt that his daughters were adequately safe-guarded against all eventualities – such was the value of the pound sterling in those days and the confident expectation that this happy state of affairs would continue indefinitely.

## Uganda: a flapper's view: 1927–29

In the Autumn of 1927, my brother's fiancée Eva Walsh (a fellow graduate of Trinity College) and I set off for Mombasa on board a British India ship, the SS *Modasa*, suitably chaperoned by the wife of a senior East African official. Eva's travels had hitherto been confined to Europe so she was understandably rather at a loss in trying to imagine what Africa would be like. I can remember her asking me if Entebbe would be similar to a small Irish town. Dredging through my memories of Nyasaland, I came up with the information that it would be more like a large village, and I was to find that this description was not so far off the mark.

Nowadays we all travel so swiftly and so lightly that it is hard to believe how much thought and packing a journey to Africa entailed in 1927. Provision had to be made not only for all the personal requirements for the coming tour, but also for the variety of clothing – including several evening frocks – needed for a voyage lasting four weeks in climatic conditions ranging from cold to tropical. Everything had to be wrapped carefully in layer after layer of tissue paper in the rather vain hope of avoiding creases, for materials were very far from being easy-care in those days.

Like my parents in 1901, Eva had been lavishly endowed with wedding presents and household goods, which, mercifully, could be labelled 'NOT WANTED ON VOYAGE' and forgotten about until we disembarked at Mombasa. My own luggage comprised two cabin trunks, a large suitcase, a hatbox (also large) and – of all things – a cello; Eva's personal effects were on a similar scale, though without the musical accompaniment. Naturally we had our full quota of topis, double Terais and mosquito boots, but at least spine pads and cholera belts had gone by the board by then. It was certainly quite a job to fit our belongings and ourselves into the tiny cabin we shared.

This was the first of several similar voyages I was to make and it was by far the most enjoyable. Once I had recovered from the ravages induced by the Bay of Biscay, I was completely carefree and had a delightful time as the youngest member of the young set. This was the heyday of the 'flapper' and, with our shingled heads, cloche hats and skimpy waistless frocks, we thought we were very dashing and sophisticated, though I for one was as naïve and imma-ture as a newly hatched chicken.

The weeks at sea flashed past, with trips ashore providing a little variety. Port Said, with its spurious curios and persistent gilli-gilli men, was specially new and exciting to me. Less enjoyable were three sweltering days spent loading coal at Port Sudan where, although all portholes were tightly closed, everything became coated with black dust. In general though I had settled so happily into the tiny microcosm of life on board ship that our arrival at Mombasa was something of an anticlimax. Here the humidity and the palm trees reminded me of the West Indies and, as we wilted under the corrugated iron roof of the customs' shed, I wondered uneasily if this was a foretaste of what awaited me in Uganda, which, after all, lay astride the equator.

It was quite a relief when the time came to board the train that was to take us via Nairobi to Kisumu (at that time known as Port Florence) on Lake Victoria – a journey last-ing two whole days. The compartments were roomy, with wide slippery seats, which were made up as bunks at night. As the train puffed its way up to the highlands, it became extremely cold and we were glad of the heavy blankets that were provided in the bed-rolls we hired at five shillings a time. There was no restaurant car so at meal times we stopped at stations that consisted of little more than a tin shack and a pile of timber for our wood-burning engine. But surprisingly good meals were produced, as if by magic, and we were glad of the opportunity to stretch our legs before resuming our journey.

We woke next morning to a very different landscape of scrub and thorn trees. Where modern travellers are regaled with a couple of full-length films to while away the tedium of a trans-Atlantic flight, we enjoyed a 'live' show of animals in their natural habitat. We saw buck in many varieties, ostriches, zebra and giraffe – the latter with their rocking-horse movement looking as if they had emerged from an enormous toy box. Elephants seemed to keep well away from the railway and on this occasion we saw no lions. On later journeys I was to see lions lying quite unconcernedly near the track, but they blended so well with the general colour scheme that it took someone with a seeing eye to point them out.

The train was still an object of great interest to the local population who waved cheerfully as we passed and who frequented the stations merely for the pleasure of gazing with unabashed curiosity at the passengers. No doubt we in our garments looked as peculiar to them as they and their lack thereof did to us. Such 'clothing' as was worn were chiefly bits of greasy leather and coils of wire around limbs and neck; a further decorative effect was achieved by piercing and stretching earlobes so that they dangled in loops at shoulder-length. There were certainly no pioneers of Women's Liberation among the girls who, from the age of about five, were all bent double under heavy loads that were suspended from straps worn around the forehead.

We reached Nairobi towards noon that second day and found that it was a big city by East African standards, though the majority of shops and offices were made of corrugated iron. There was a saying at that time that there was nothing more permanent than Nairobi's temporary buildings! Certainly, the large unofficial element on the Legislative Council saw to it that money was not wasted on grandiose government establishments and the like.

The area around Nairobi could have had little to recommend it to the early developers, for it was mainly flat and swampy. But it at least had the virtue of providing level ground where the railway's engineers could build workshops and assemble rolling stock and materials before embarking on their daunting task of constructing the line up the escarpment of the Rift Valley and on towards Lake Victoria. As this work was proceeding, an increasing number of would-be farmers were arriving from the United Kingdom and from South Africa, all eager to take up land in the highlands. So the administration was obliged, willy-nilly, to move up from Mombasa. The ever-enterprising Indians were not slow in opening up *duka*s (shops) and very soon Nairobi was well on the way to becoming a sizeable town, destined to emerge as the fine city it is today.

Nairobi was our chaperone's destination and she and her husband, who met us, very kindly took us to their house for lunch and a much needed wash and brush up. One of the trials of the journey was that the line was still unmetalled and passengers and their belongings quickly became coated in red dust. The residential area was at a higher level than the shops and offices, and the bungalows in their shady gardens were very cool and pleasant – I began to feel more hopeful about conditions in Uganda.

After lunch Eva and I continued our journey, climbing steadily through the highlands and skirting the spectacular Rift Valley until the engine – sounding as if it were breathing its last – reached Mau Summit, which at 9000 feet was

46

the highest point on the line. After that we descended more than 5000 feet to Kisumu where a little ship called the *Clement Hill* was waiting to take the Uganda passengers on the final overnight stage of their journey.

Since the Second World War most people's first view of Entebbe has been through the porthole of an aircraft. But I am glad that my own first glimpse of this very beautiful place was from the water by the clear light of an African dawn. As I had surmised, it had the appearance of a large and exotic village, for green tree-shaded lawns sloped down to the sandy fringes of the lake and shrubs and creepers in vibrant colours grew in profusion out of the rich, red soil.

On that early morning towards the end of November 1927, Entebbe had the rather unreal look of a modern travel poster. There was, too, something of the Sleeping Beauty in the scene. I was soon to find that appearances were not deceptive, for the abode of the very senior official was irreverently known as 'Sleepy Hollow'.

My parents' house was an old, rambling bungalow with rooms leading out of each other and the whole building enclosed in mosquito wire, which made it look rather like a large meat safe. None of us seemed to think it strange that, more than a quarter of a century after my parents' first arrival in Africa, living conditions were every bit as primitive as they had been before. The inconveniences were all unquestionably taken for granted as being an inescapable part of life in Africa, though to some extent they were offset by a staff of about seven indoor servants, plus three *shamba* (garden) boys and a chauffeur. When my parents came to Uganda in 1921, rickshaws were still in general use but cars soon took over, though in Nairobi rickshaws with their plumed operators were still available for hire well into the 1940s.

At first everything seemed very new and exciting, particularly since we were preparing for the wedding of my brother and Eva, which was naturally the big social event of

7. Charles and Aileen Griffin's household staff, Entebbe, Uganda. How did they manage? 1920s.

the year. After that, however, life began to seem very boring indeed for I was entirely lacking in companionship of my own age and was without any useful or interesting pursuits.

Time hung very heavy on my hands – all the more so as there was an unwritten law, which governs me even to this day, that one could not read a book before lunch; newspapers were permitted but at that time in Uganda this was no more than a once-weekly folded sheet. One could get away with one of the more solid magazines – also in short supply – but anything else was frowned on.

After lunch when, in accordance with custom, my mother and I retired to rest from the heat if not from our labours, I could at last enjoy a good read. Then there was a slight respite from the general monotony after tea when it was cool enough for golf and tennis. But even there I felt the lack of contemporaries, for my partners and opponents were mostly married people, years older than I was, and no doubt very kind to bother about me at all.

Entertaining consisted almost exclusively of formal dinner parties, with five courses followed by a port session for the men. How our servants produced those elaborate meals with the most rudimentary equipment is amazing enough, but even more amazing is that we took their achievements entirely for granted. After-dinner entertainment involved card games or music, and I blush to recall with what smug self-satisfaction I played and sang for the benefit of an indulgent, middle-aged audience.

Meals were always fairly formal and even for the most casual potluck supper one could count on three courses. On one of these occasions our cook was drunk and the meal was a disaster. Next morning when remonstrating with the culprit my mother said, 'Just suppose that had happened at a real dinner party,' whereupon he drew himself up and reminded her severely that he would never get drunk if there were more than eight to dinner!

One potluck visitor, however, came in for very special treatment. When a shy young clergyman appeared at the door, obviously under the impression that he was expected for dinner even although his hosts had actually finished their meal and were thinking of going to bed, the lady of the house was undaunted. His kind-hearted if somewhat eccentric hostess welcomed him warmly and apologized that dinner would be a little late owing to some misadventure in the back premises. Pressing a sherry into his hand and giving her husband a conspiratorial look, she hurried outside to confer with her cook who thereupon proceeded to catch, kill and roast a chicken, which was duly consumed with varying degrees of enthusiasm.

Entebbe's social highlight was a monthly dance at the club, but these events would be wrecked if they coincided with the full moon, for this inevitably signalled the arrival of millions of lake flies. These insects did not bite or sting, but they had a slightly fishy smell and were all pervading, clogging the senses, getting into the food and drink, and even endangering the safety of drivers and pedestrians.

To begin with, at any rate, the climate came as a pleasant surprise because, although it was always very hot and humid around the middle of the day, the temperature rarely rose above the eighties. However, I was soon to find that the lack of seasonal change was trying in itself, and I once heard the situation well summed up by someone who remarked that for the first three months Uganda's climate was heavenly but after that it was simply boring.

One event that stands out from those early months in Uganda was when the Cobhams, an intrepid husband and wife team, landed their tiny seaplane on the lake near Entebbe. I was among the small crowd that saw them being paddled ashore in a dugout canoe to a very informal reception, at which the only official presence was the governor's aide-de-camp who had come to take them to Government House for the night. We were full of admiration for their courage in venturing so far in their frail craft, but I doubt if any of us realized that they were blazing a trail that even the least adventurous of us would be following as a matter of course in the not too distant future.

When I look back to the days of my youth from my busy seventies, what strikes me most about that time were the boredom and idleness of middle-class women both at home and abroad. Living now in a virtually classless society, it is hard to believe how sharply the social barriers were defined before the Second World War, and what a stultifying effect this had on middle-class women who had few intellectual outlets and for whom any form of housework other than a little cake making and flower arranging was absolutely taboo. As a friend said to me recently, 'We could clean the church brasses but not our own silver!'

In tropical Africa, admittedly, we could hardly have been expected to cope with the wood-burning cooker or scrub the cement floors, but there must surely have been lighter domestic tasks that could have provided us with a little pleasurable diversion.

As I have already said, my mother was a gifted home-maker and was at heart an extremely practical person who, had she belonged to a different 'class' or lived in a later era, could have coped successfully with household chores and would have been all the happier for doing so. Certainly, her house ran on oiled wheels and, in view of the number of servants, one is tempted to say 'and well it might'. Yet I think she must be given the credit for instilling high standards of cleanliness and order and for being a good employer, for where some *memsahibs* perpetually seemed to be hiring and firing, she rarely made changes in her staff.

Apart from taking over the cake making – an almost daily occupation because there were frequent callers at tea-time – there was really nothing for me to do. My mother's housekeeping amounted largely to an after-breakfast session with her cook. She ordered the day's meals and told him what to fetch from the market with the assistance of his *toto*, who invariably accompanied him on these expeditions. Meanwhile, the pantry-*toto* was dispatched with a chit to fetch such groceries as were needed from one of the little Indian *dukas*.

When my father's work took him to Kampala, a distance of about 23 miles along a dusty, winding road, my mother and I generally also went to avail ourselves of its superior shopping facilities, though these only amounted to a couple of European-owned shops dealing mainly in provisions and hardware with a small line in clothing and soft furnishings, and a few Indian curio shops. There was also quite a good bookshop run by the Church Missionary Society – though non-sectarian as regards stock – which was much patronized by my father.

A big event in our life was the appearance every few

months of the *box-wallah*, an itinerant Indian who travelled around the country with porters carrying boxes of silken materials. He would spread out a sheet on the veranda and, with infinite patience, display his wares, which always smelled exotically of sandalwood. As all underwear was homemade in those days and tended to wear out quickly in the tropics, his patience was almost invariably rewarded.

In the late 1920s the British in Uganda numbered a mere 1000. Apart from missionaries, among whom other European nationalities were included, and the personnel of banks and a few commercial firms, the majority were civil servants and their wives and families. These were strictly divided between senior and junior officials, and ne'er the twain did meet outside office hours. Very occasionally someone rose from the ranks, but where today we would applaud his enterprise and industry he was then regarded as 'jumped up' and out of his proper milieu. In general, we looked down on the commercial sector, though the manager of the National Bank of India seemed to rank as a sort of honorary senior official.

Our living conditions may have been primitive but there was great formality with regard to such things as precedence and visiting cards. Everyone had to sign the Government House 'book' at regular intervals and 'calling' on newcomers was compulsory, though they were expected to call first on the chief justice's and chief secretary's households. Every *memsahib* had a 'not at home' box hung at the ready outside her front door every afternoon to receive cards, but it did not always tell the truth.

The only female civil servants at that time were a couple of doctors, the nursing sisters and the women at the telephone exchange, for it was inconceivable that a woman could be married and hold down a job. If, for instance, one of the nursing sisters wished to get married – a not infrequent occurrence – her contract was automatically terminated on the day of the nuptials. So, when a couple of years later one of the women doctors announced her intention to marry a man in the legal department and carry on her work as a pathologist, she really put the cat among the pigeons.

They were both getting on in years, so it was unlikely that the patter of little feet would take her mind off the job, but there were endless deliberations before her request received very reluctant consent. It was not until the Second World War, when there was a shortage of personnel, that married women were allowed to work as nurses, teachers and secretaries, though generally only on a part-time basis, whereas an increasing number of unmarried women were being appointed to full-time positions in the education, medical and community development departments.

The governor, whose attractive Palladian-style colonial residence appropriately looked down over the rest of us, must have led an extremely boring social existence. Although, as one Scottish lady put it, all senior officials expected to get their knees under his mahogany at least once a year and the rest were invited to an annual garden party, he, by some strange convention, was only supposed to dine with the chief justice and chief secretary. If, as was all too likely to be the case, he and these dignitaries were not on particularly good terms, it was just too bad.

At one Government House dinner party that same Scottish lady became the victim of a practical joke: during dinner her feet were killing her so she eased them out of her shoes; the bright young spark sitting next to her who noted this manoeuvre, promptly kicked them out of her reach so that when the time came for the ladies to retire she had to make a flat-footed exit.

In general, life was uneventful and perhaps it was because of this that there was always a sense of hopeful expectancy among the higher echelon as the time for Birthday and New Year honours came around. In fact there were few surprises, for everyone had a fairly good idea of what – if anything – lay in store.

Governors were knighted either on appointment or soon afterwards and chief justices could confidently expect their knighthood within a few years of attaining this status. Chief secretaries and directors of medical services (known at that time as principal medical officers) were awarded the CMG, usually when they were about to retire, while the CBE was bestowed on the heads of other departments.

Soon after the Second World War there were some changes in this procedure, with chief secretaries sometimes qualifying for knighthoods and permanent secretaries receiving the CMG or CBE, while a few governors actually became life peers. There were even a few out-of-the-way knighthoods to liven up the scene and, at a less exalted level, there was occasional recognition for special services, as in the case of my husband whose OBE was, I am sure, more because he was chairman of public health on the Kampala municipality and had been actively involved in the East African Medical Association and various other concerns than for his long years and hard work in the medical department.[1]

A few Africans, including the *Kabaka* Sir Daudi Chwa, were also honoured. His *katikiro* (prime minister) Apolo Kagwa was inadvertently awarded the same distinction when the cable containing the Honours List referred to him as Apolo K CMG. But, although clearly an error, the award could not be rescinded without causing great offence.

Of the four races that made up the population of Uganda, the natives were of course by far the most

---

1. My mother heard of our father's award from another source. When asked why he had not told her the news, he replied that he had received a letter but it was marked 'confidential'. With equal modesty, my mother also omitted to record that she was later awarded the MBE for her services to the community (editor).

numerous, but they were also the least assertive. The word 'native' has acquired a derogatory connotation, but it is hard to know how otherwise to refer to Uganda's indigenous population, for it is composed of many tribes. The term 'Ugandan', coined at the time of independence in 1962, cannot even now be said to describe a close-knit national group. Indeed, the ink of that carefully worked-out constitution had barely dried before tribal rivalries and enmities, kept in check by the British presence – and not, be it noted, by force – once more reared their heads with tragic consequences for the country and all its peoples.

From my memory, at least, the Africans – as perhaps I had better refer to them – seemed in those pre-Second World War days to be basking in a sort of indolent contentment and, if any stirrings of political ambition lurked beneath the placid waters of their existence, they were certainly very well concealed. In general, their needs were few and simple; and they had not yet experienced the pressures and dissatisfactions that seem to be the inevitable fruits of civilization. Uganda's status as a protectorate rather than a colony presumably implied ultimate self-government, but I doubt very much if anyone – black or white – expected such a development in the foreseeable future.

Those who are unfamiliar with East Africa do not always realize that Buganda is merely one of Uganda's four provinces, though it happens to be the one in which both Entebbe and Kampala, the government and commercial hubs respectively, are situated. The people of Buganda are known as the Baganda, and the *Kabaka* was their hereditary ruler.

The declining fortunes and tragic death of Daudi's successor, Mutesa (King Freddy), the last of the dynasty, are well known, but when I came to Uganda in 1927 he was a very small boy. His father held sway within the constraints of the Buganda Agreement and the royal residence, in a group of rather superior huts surrounded by a fence of elaborately woven cane, was situated on a hill near Kampala called Mengo. Once a year, on the *Kabaka*'s birthday, he played host, unwillingly I imagine, to all and sundry at a garden party and on the first of these occasions I attended I saw little Mutesa most uncomfortably clad, *à la* Little Lord Fauntleroy, in blue velvet.

Normally, the different races kept to themselves and clubs, for instance, were clearly labelled 'European', 'Indian' and 'Goan'. The only evidence of African social life came at night when drumbeats resounding from *shamba*s outside the townships told that *ngoma*s (beer parties cum dances) were in progress. On only one occasion can I recall an African other than a servant in my parents' house and this was when an interpreter from the High Court came to see my father on an official matter; he was a good-looking young man and a member of one of Buganda's leading families. He spoke excellent English and was neatly dressed in a spotless *kanzu* (a long garment rather like a nightshirt) and European-style jacket. But at the time it was quite extraordinary to see him sitting on a chair in my parents' drawing room.

The Baganda were then the most educationally advanced people in the country; they were a handsome lot and looked well fed. The word 'comely' seems particularly descriptive of the women's glossy and curvaceous attractions, which were much enhanced by their style of dress: this comprised a full-length garment formed from a long piece of material, which was wound tightly under the arms and pleated in at the waist, where it was somehow held together by a wide sash. More often than not a baby would be tucked in at the small of the back, and very sweet it looked too, with its curly little head bobbing about while mother got on with cultivating the *shamba* or any other chores.

The African mud huts stood in shady groves of plantain trees and had such a charmingly appropriate appearance that it almost seemed as if they, too, had grown out of the fertile soil. They were reasonably hygienic also, for if a hut became dilapidated or infested it could easily be demolished and cheaply replaced. Already, however, there was a tendency to build European-style houses, which were much more costly to build and maintain and very quickly brought a note of squalor to what had been an idyllic rural setting.

At that time there had been no real influx to the townships, so most people lived in the traditional manner on their *shamba*s where they grew most of their food and also produced cotton, which was the country's main export and source of revenue. To some extent it might be said that their clothes grew on the trees, for bark cloth was still preferred over shop-bought material for special occasions. Much time and patience went into preparing bark cloth: it had first to be carefully stripped off the tree and then very gently hammered out to the required size and texture. The finished article was rather like coarse linen in a rich shade of tan and looked very good against an African skin. But, as it tore very easily and could not be washed, it was unsuited to general use. Men also favoured bark cloth robes for 'best', but the more practical European styles were rapidly gaining in favour. Houseboys (there were no female servants other than *ayah*s) wore a *kanzu*, with a coloured cummerbund and short waistcoat to smarten the effect.

The Goans were yet another component of the population and without their clerical services many a government department would have ground to a halt. A few owned shops, while others worked as tailors, for there was constant demand for cotton suits and frocks, but, in general, Goans did not go in for big business. They were highly respectable people and devout Catholics who took great pride in their Portuguese ancestry and religious tradition. For them Goa was 'home', the place they visited on leave and where they hoped to end their days, so India's annexation of their homeland must have come as a terrible shock.

The Indians, as everyone from that subcontinent were

known in those days, far outstripped the other races in industry and enterprise. From a numerically small, humble start as labourers on the railways, they were developing into an increasingly important force in the commercial life of East Africa.

The many shopkeepers and craftsmen among them (who were all referred to as *fundis*) were one and all prepared to endure a very low standard of living until they had made their pile. Gradually, they bought up plots in the developing townships and acquired land that was turned into flourishing sugar estates. They also owned and operated the cotton ginneries that played such an important part in the country's economy. Later, when they numbered several professional men and had become prominent in public affairs, the wealthiest among them vied with each other to build grandiose homes on Kampala's suburban hillsides. Inevitably, one heard about them exploiting Africans and undoubtedly there was a certain amount of truth in this, but we should not forgot that it was Asian initiative, hard work and financial investment that contributed so much to the general level of prosperity in Uganda.

Life in the early 1920s was pretty easy going for senior officials in Entebbe. However, when Sir William Gowers was appointed governor in 1926 he soon set about stirring them out of their lethargy and cared not at all that he made himself unpopular in the process.

Probably the main examples of progress on the part of government were to be seen on two hills on the outskirts of Kampala where Makerere College and Mulago Hospital had recently come into being. Mulago was originally started by Major Gerald Keane DSO as a clinic for the treatment of VD, but it was developing rapidly into a large general hospital and was soon to provide teaching facilities for both doctors and nurses. Later the medical school became part of Makerere College, which eventually achieved full university status with affiliation to London University.

It was, however, the missionaries, both Protestant and Catholic, who were the pioneers in the fields of both education and medicine. In their simple and selfless way of life they were far closer to the Africans and had a better understanding of their needs than the vast majority of government officials. An exception was the old-style district officers who had the welfare of the people in their charge very much at heart and were loved and respected in return. Paternalism is now much decried but in this case and at that time it was a mutually beneficial relationship.

Despite my admiration for the missionaries, I have always felt that it must have been confusing in the extreme for the Africans to be offered two – or even more – brands of Christianity and to sense the rivalry and even, in earlier days, the enmity that existed between the different factions, which all proclaimed the doctrine of brotherly love.

The main Catholic and Protestant strongholds, Rubaga and Namirembi, were on imposing hilltop sites near Kampala, from which the respective cathedrals, one Italianate in style and the other like a red brick version of St Paul's, faced each other across the valley. Adjacent to the cathedrals, and at every mission centre throughout the country, there were schools and hospitals, for the people's educational, physical and spiritual wellbeing were all part of the missionary's endeavour. Both cathedrals had been built with the active cooperation of their believers who would carry bricks as they climbed the steep hillsides to attend their respective Sunday services. Both denominations had many faithful adherents and on wet Sunday mornings it looked as if large green caterpillars were on the move as hundreds of churchgoers wended their way uphill under 'umbrellas' made of banana leaves.

Both denominations numbered many unsung heroes and heroines but just a few came to be well known beyond Uganda's borders. Dr (later Sir) Albert Cook of the Church Missionary Society was one of the earliest medical missionaries to walk up from the coast in the 1880s and give a lifetime of service to the people of Uganda.

Among the Catholics, Mother Kevin of the Franciscan Sisters inaugurated hospitals, maternity centres and leper colonies, and became a byword for energy and enterprise. When I first came to Uganda the principal medical officer was Major Keane, whom I have already mentioned. He was a Catholic and a very fine man in many ways, but he had an inordinate fear of appearing to favour his own kind; in consequence, he tended to lean in the other direction. Mother Kevin was once heard to exclaim in a moment of exasperation that she prayed his successor would be a 'decent Protestant'.

Another pioneer, though of a very different sort, was Michael Moses, an Armenian from Baghdad who as a very young man had been enthralled by tales of the fortunes in 'white gold' (elephant tusks) that awaited an intrepid traveller to East Africa. Having, like the missionaries, endured the trials and tribulations of walking up from the coast, his arrival in Kampala coincided with the outbreak of the Sudanese mutiny. Before he had time to recover from the ravages of his journey, he was dispatched as Her Majesty Queen Victoria's rather unlikely representative to the Hoima district with instructions to keep the peace at all costs.

He found a tense situation – the troops under his command were in two minds about whether or not to join their mutineering brothers – and much depended on this inexperienced young Armenian whose life was imperilled keeping up an appearance of unruffled calm. Somehow he remained in control of the situation and the crisis passed. But offers of employment by an appreciative government held no attraction for one of his independent and adventurous spirit, and he was soon deeply involved in the ivory trade and in other such lucrative propositions as came his way.

For several years his life was one long arduous safari,

during which he covered on foot vast areas extending into the Belgian Congo. As money became available, he bought building plots in the developing townships and plantations on which he pioneered some of Uganda's most important crops. When I first knew him he was a power in the land – the 'uncrowned king' whose counsel was sought by those in high places. He was friendly with my parents and, in due course, was to become very attached to me and to my family to whom he was almost embarrassingly kind and generous.

My father was always loath to leave the comforts of his home, but from time to time his duties took him on safari, as even the most prosaic journey was termed. I was disappointed that he did not take his family with him on these occasions, but this was largely explained by the fact that he was either put up by the local magistrate or district officer, on whose hospitality he did not wish to presume, or had to endure the discomforts of a rest house.

My horizons were narrow, so I was delighted when my former chaperone and her husband came to Uganda in the course of his duties as Postmaster-General (of the East African territories). They invited me to accompany them to Fort Portal in the Toro district, lying beneath the famous Mountains of the Moon, which crown the Ruwenzori range.

Fort Portal is about 220 miles from Entebbe and it was a rather tedious journey through a mainly featureless countryside. Except in the more arid eastern and extreme northern provinces, Uganda is almost overpoweringly green and lush, due largely to elephant grass and papyrus swamps, but although the lakeside views are very beautiful the landscape in general is uninspiring. Later I was to find that the most spectacular scenery was in the western Kigezi district, which is an area of lakes and mountains bordering the Congo. As we neared our destination, however, conical hills, presumably of volcanic origin, relieved the monotony and the countryside became more interesting. The people we passed by the roadside reminded me of the Kikuyu I had seen when travelling through Kenya, though their comparable living conditions could have explained the similarities in their appearance and 'dress'. With their rudimentary little huts looking like beehives perched precariously on the hillsides, they would had to have had wiry physiques in order to cultivate their steep little *shamba*s.

In Fort Portal we stayed at what was then the only hotel – inevitably named the 'Mountains of the Moon' – which faced the Ruwenzori range. But only on one occasion did those dazzlingly beautiful peaks emerge from the mist in which they sometimes remain hidden for weeks on end. I was once told that the explorer Henry Stanley spent quite a long time in this neighbourhood without being aware that those snowy slopes existed.

I visited Toro again some months later, this time under the wing of the acting governor Mr Rankine and his wife, so I was making right royal progress African style. *En route* we spent a night at the Mityana rest camp where the police sergeant was so determined to show His (Acting) Excellency due respect that he turned out a guard of honour every time the poor man tried to make an unobtrusive visit to the pit latrine.

Toro is renowned for game of every description, but none came my way on either of these occasions. Indeed, the only wild animal I encountered during my early years in Uganda was virtually tame. This was a crocodile known as Lutembe, whose photographs in the *Illustrated London News* had brought it world fame. I was one of the first to see the crocodile being put through its paces by a fisherman who had somehow acquired the monopoly of this ageing beast.

I went at dawn with some friends to a spot on the lake shore midway between Entebbe and Kampala where, having extracted black-market rates for fish for his protégé, the fisherman proceeded to summon the crocodile to its feast by repeated calls of 'Lutembe! Lutembe!' A faint ripple on the lake surface gradually widened and soon the loathsome looking animal heaved itself onto the beach and lay facing us expectantly. One by one the fish were thrown into its snapping jaws and, when it was obvious that no more were forthcoming, it returned to the water with its guardian holding up its tail in the manner of a trainbearer. It was an astonishing display and one I was to see repeated on several occasions over the next few years, for a visit to Lutembe became a popular family outing at weekends. But gradually his appearances became less predictable and eventually he was seen no more.

Wild animals were, indeed, seen so rarely near the main roads that there was a saying that the most dangerous one likely to be encountered was a White Father on his *piki-piki*!

In general, life continued to be uneventful. I can remember saying to my mother that when we went on leave I would like to take a course in kindergarten teaching with a view to doing something for the small children in Entebbe and providing myself with a little interesting occupation. Her reply was hardly encouraging: 'I doubt if your father would let you, my dear!' Fortunately, before we came to blows, life took on a different aspect, for my future husband Dr Arthur Boase, hitherto unknown to my family, was transferred to Entebbe from the Eastern Province.

Arthur also had a colonial background as his father was in the British Guiana medical service and he too had been left 'at home' – in England in his case – for schooling, which was followed by medical training at St Thomas' Hospital in London. When he qualified in 1924 he joined the colonial medical service and was posted to Uganda. Unlike the legal service, in which personnel tended to move from one end of the globe to the other, doctors were appointed to one specific colony or protectorate and usually remained there for the whole of their service, though there was a good deal of exchange at head office level between the different East African territories and this applied to other departments too.

Only many years later were there some transfers further afield and Arthur was offered – and declined – the post of ophthalmic specialist in the Gold Coast. Like most raw recruits, on arrival he was thrown in at the deep end by having a spell at Mulago Hospital where a bewildering variety of medical and surgical conditions confronted him; he probably learnt more in a few short weeks there than he had done throughout his years as a student.

He was then dispatched on his *piki-piki* to his first upcountry station, Arua in the West Nile. This was a journey by road and water, which took days or weeks depending on how lucky one was in connecting with lake and river steamers. It must have been a daunting experience for one so recently qualified to find himself, on arrival, entirely on his own professionally. But those weeks at Mulago had at least given him an insight into what to expect.

The hospital at Arua was extremely primitive, consisting mainly of a group of thatched and whitewashed mud huts. The patients' ailments generally ranged from blackwater fever, dysentery and pneumonia to wounds inflicted by man and beast. Surgery could only be performed on an emergency basis as the doctor had to be his own anaesthetist, handing over the chloroform bottle to an orderly as soon as the patient was 'under' so that he could get on with the job as quickly as possible. At that time it was believed that ether, which is so much safer than chloroform, could not be used in the tropics because of the danger of evaporation and some years were to pass before this theory was disproved.

There were no wonder drugs in those days and quinine,

aspirin, castor oil, Epsom salts and iodine had to meet most needs, though the medicine cupboard also contained a supply of brandy and champagne to be used as a last resort, though I think they were occasionally broached in less extreme circumstances.

After some months in this outpost, Arthur was transferred back to Mulago where he remained until the end of his tour. On return from leave he was posted to the Eastern Province for a short spell in Mbale and a longer one in Lira. After this he was brought to headquarters in Entebbe and given the task of writing the medical department's annual report. At that point, in 1928, our stories converged.

The starting salary for a doctor in 1924, when Arthur joined, was £600 a year; cadets in the administration regarded them with some envy because they then received a mere £300. There was some justice in this, however, for a doctor's training took at least five years – at their parents' expense – and they were generally a couple of years older than the cadets were on appointment. In these inflationary days it is interesting to note how slowly the value of money changed during the first quarter of this century; new administrative recruits in 1927 (when my brother joined) started at £400 – only £100 better off than my father had been when he went to Nyasaland in 1901. There was still no income tax to pay and, to the best of everyone's belief, the purchasing power of the pound sterling would remain the same this year, next year and *ad infinitum*.

Newcomers to the service were expected to pass a fairly basic exam in Swahili or Luganda before their appointment was confirmed, though I never heard of one that was not, and further linguistic efforts were rewarded with a bonus of £50, which was a very pleasant windfall in those days. It was a pity that wives were not given similar encouragement, for it was all too easy to get away with something referred to as 'Kiswa *memsahib*'. I doubt if my mother knew half a dozen words of either Swahili or Luganda, and her cook's knowledge of English was of a similar standard. But I must admit they managed to understand each other very well and to this day a Madeira cake is known in our family as a 'cherry cake *hapana* (without) cherry'!

There are certain words that all ex-East Africans use constantly: for instance *maridadi* in expressing the highest praise for someone's appearance, behaviour or workmanship and *shenzi* for a corresponding degree of disgust, contempt or dissatisfaction; *pole-pole* and *pesi-pesi* respectively for slowly or carefully and quickly or get a move on! *Kali sana* is either very hot or very fierce, and *shauri* covers an argument, a bit of business or bother or, quite simply, a topic of conversation. *Katibwa* is in a class of its own, but in so far as it can be translated it implies prestige, kudos or *amour propre*, while the Luganda word *magezi* merely means common sense.

In due course Arthur and I became engaged and our wedding was planned to take place early in April 1929 when his leave was due. Meanwhile, many afternoons were devoted to my driving lessons, which took place among the anthills of an otherwise level area that eventually became Entebbe's international airport. Arthur was my instructor and we were not the first to learn that emotional involvement is no help – to put it mildly – in such matters and I achieved little in the way of proficiency and confidence.

There seemed to be an undeniable inevitability about embarking on married life in Africa, for it was very much in the family tradition. Yet, I was not unduly enamoured of the tropics and was destined always to be immune to the fascination Africa exercises over so many expatriates.

Meanwhile, Entebbe was working up to a visit by the Prince of Wales in the autumn of 1928 – an event that caused far more excitement than the Cobhams' momentous visit had done earlier in the year. For weeks before he arrived, the subject of clothes loomed large on feminine horizons and there was much speculation over who would be invited to what. Postal shopping became the order of the day and an evening dress was ordered for me from one of Nairobi's few 'exclusive' shops. It at least had the distinction of giving Entebbe its first glimpse of the latest fashion, being short in front and swooping to lower calf-length at the back.

My parents were among the small group presented to the Prince when he stepped off the *Clement Hill*, while the rest of us kept our distance. The Africans who had turned out in considerable numbers were disappointed by the prince's unassuming appearance. Although the governor was in all his glory of gold lace and plumed hat, His Royal Highness was clad in a very plain, rather crumpled khaki uniform – just like my father's chauffeur according to one of our servants.

We dined at Government House that night and there was an informal dance afterwards at which, I must hasten to say, I did not dance with the Prince of Wales who, understandably, was not interested in *ingénues*. Next day we attended a vast garden party, but as soon as those social obligations were over the prince made a thankful escape to the broad open spaces in search of big game. It is, I think, worth noting that in this era, before 'shooting' with cameras happily replaced the use of guns, many a government official paid for his children's schooling by bagging a good pair of tusks. As it turned out, the Prince's safari had to be cut short when he was recalled to England because of George V's serious illness.

Uganda was singularly lacking in honeymoon spots. The only hotels were the Mountains of the Moon – already mentioned and less romantic than it sounds – the Imperial in Kampala, which was no great shakes, and a small establishment in Tororo in the Eastern Province, where Mein Host was a bit of a martinet and charged extra if his guests did not have a bath! So, although a few hardy souls braved the discomforts of rest camps in the cause of togetherness and some took themselves off to Hudson-Cain's country club in the Kenya Highlands, others, including ourselves, timed the nuptials to coincide with the start of home leave.

In our case we elected to spend ten days in Zanzibar before joining the *Llandovery Castle* for the voyage to England. So, after our wedding in the White Fathers' church in Entebbe, our journey began with the usual crossing of Lake Victoria on the *Clement Hill*. On this we were allotted the royal suite, which had been prepared for the Duke and Duchess of York (later George VI and Queen Elizabeth) when they visited East Africa a few years before – and also used, I presume, by the Prince of Wales more recently. At Kisumu we boarded the train for what should have been a 30-hour trip to Mombasa, but during the night we ran off the rails!

It was hardly an auspicious start to married life, but no damage was done to either train or passengers except that we were left high and dry without food (apart for some wedding cake) for several hours until a breakdown train could come to our rescue. Our main anxiety was that we would miss the British India boat that was to take us to Zanzibar. But, eventually, we scrambled on board at the eleventh hour, looking and feeling incredibly filthy but otherwise none the worse for our adventure.

We enjoyed our ten days in Zanzibar very much and were fortunate to have the relative comfort of a seaside bungalow, complete with private beach, belonging to the Sultan – those were the days! We were fascinated by the old town with its narrow streets and fine old Arab houses; it seemed so sleepy and peaceful that it was hard to believe it had been the scene of so much misery and suffering during the period of the slave trade. Nor could we have guessed that, beneath the seemingly placid surface, the memory of those horrors would live on to find expression in an appalling massacre in the latter half of the 1960s in which the slave traders' descendants paid a heavy price for their forebears' infamy.

Idyllic though our honeymoon setting had been, it unfortunately contained a hidden menace, for a few days after boarding the *Llandovery Castle* for the homeward voyage I went down with a severe attack of malaria. This was my first experience of the illness and I found it very unpleasant.

For the benefit of those who have never had malaria and tend to toss it off as 'a touch of fever', I should explain that the initial feeling of general malaise is rapidly succeeded by an icy, tooth-chattering rigor and then by a raging headache and soaring temperature. Most attacks were what was known as 'tertian', so the second day brought a slight respite from the acute symptoms only to have them return with hardly diminished force on the third, and so on. Then (and for many years to come) quinine, orally or by injection, was the only cure and this caused screaming ears and varying degrees of deafness. I believe I was laid up for over a week and then emerged as weak as a kitten and so much reduced in weight that I kept losing my newly acquired wedding ring!

In Uganda the normal tour lasted 30 months and leave entitlement was reckoned at the rate of five days for each of these months, plus a total of 60 days' travelling time, so most people were away for a period of seven months in all. Eagerly though leave was anticipated, it rarely lived up to expectations, for most of us had to rely on the hospitality of relatives or friends, or find ourselves furnished accommodation. Of course, when there were children, all this became much more complicated and expensive. I think there were few of us who did not breathe a sigh of relief as we climbed the gangway for the return journey. This in itself was probably the best part of the holiday for it was marvellous to know that for four whole weeks free board and lodging lay ahead of us.

The first leave after our marriage lasted even longer because doctors were encouraged to take additional study leave, on full pay, to gain further experience and qualifications. Arthur had become very interested in ophthal-mology, so he spent some months working in the eye department of St Thomas' Hospital. Looking back, I think I must have been mad not to have taken this heaven-sent opportunity to have cookery lessons, or even to learn to type, but the notion that I would need such skills and have to acquire them the hard way never crossed my mind. My only achievement was that I had professional driving lessons and passed the very rudimentary test, which was all that was required of drivers in those days. Only a few years previously a friend of ours in Uganda had been given a hand-written document that empowered him to drive all mechanical vehicles except aeroplanes!

We were away from Uganda for nine months in all and, on our return, we found ourselves posted to Masaka in Buganda Province.

# 2
# Arthur and Alice Boase: Uganda 1929–56

M asaka was a small but pleasant station about 90 miles from Kampala. Having collected Arthur's head boy and engaged a cook, we put them in charge of our household goods, which were to make their way by lorry. Then we set off in the Austin 12, which had travelled out from England with us. Government advanced the purchase price of cars, which were of course essential since there was no other form of transport. In our case the advance amounted, I believe, to £350 to be repaid in monthly instalments over the coming tour.

### Young family in Uganda: 1930–39

Uganda was fortunate in having murram for its roads, which were passable, however corrugated, in all seasons, unlike those in neighbouring Kenya, which were reduced in the rains to a sea of slithery mud. Our journey to Masaka took about three hours and at one point the road crossed a large swamp, which was sometimes, but not on this occasion, virtually awash during the rains.

Apart from the existence of cars, which enabled us to get about more easily, our living conditions were very similar to those my parents had encountered in Nyasaland nearly 30 years earlier – although thankfully we were spared the rats

71

and calico ceilings. Actually, our bungalow was one of a small number known as the Hesketh Bell type, which being L-shaped were slightly less box-like than most. Hesketh Bell had been an early governor, so I cannot imagine how he came to be involved in architecture, though that is perhaps too distinguished a term to use in relation to our little house, which consisted in the main of four rooms and a couple of wired-in verandas.

To the rear of every house was a group of adjoining rooms known as the 'boys' quarters. They were cell-like little apartments in which the occupant installed his own 'furniture', which usually amounted to a charpoy, a stool and a padlocked box in which he kept his belongings. There was a generally held rule that wives were not allowed to live on the premises and, indeed, the accommodation was quite inadequate for family occupation. But, although the proscription was not unduly harsh when the servant's own home was reasonably close at hand, this situation became increasingly rare as more and more men (and women) came from far afield to seek employment in the townships.

Our social attitudes have changed very much over the past 50 years, particularly since the Second World War. I was certainly not alone in being, as I now realize, quite shamefully insensitive to the hardships implicit in these family separations and to the fact that, when an *ayah* was employed, she was inevitably put into an invidious position. My own *ayah*s over the years were mature women who presumably knew how to look after themselves, but sometimes quite young girls were employed in this capacity and no doubt they were exploited – whether willingly or not.

My insensitivity was, in fact, very much part of that era and it was by no means confined to Africa or to other parts of the colonial empire. Even in so-called civilized countries, few employers concerned themselves with the private lives of their servants and it was taken for granted that they slept in comfortless attics and worked in sunless basements. Their 'followers' were banned from the vicinity of the house and, on her weekly half day, a servant fared even worse than Cinderella, for she was obliged to return by 10 p.m. – a seemingly magic hour before which 'nothing' untoward was likely to happen. Social inequalities were unquestionably accepted as part of the natural order – a view embodied in Mrs Alexander's well-known hymn 'All things bright and beautiful' – for no one, either rich or poor, saw anything strange in asserting in ringing tones that the Almighty had 'made the high, the lowly, and ordered their estate'!

There was no regular system of holidays for our African servants, although when we ourselves went on leave it was customary to pay a retainer to those who were regarded as being on the permanent staff – this generally excluded *toto*s (youngsters) who tended to come and go in the cause of bettering themselves. Obviously, servants felt the need to return home from time to time, but this was never admitted in so many words. Instead, an urgent message would be received announcing some family emergency and off the recipient would go for an indefinite period – generally depending on how soft hearted the employer was in the matter of an advance of pay to deal with the supposed crisis. Usually, and by mutual arrangement no doubt, these absences were staggered so that not too much inconvenience was involved. But at one stage, some years later, our staff seemed so catastrophe prone that I was moved to commemorate the situation in verse:

> Oh! for a houseboy quite bereft,
> With ne'er a mother nor father left,
> No one to die, no one to ail,
> No one to need an advance for bail.
>
> Never again to hear the cry –
> 'Daddy *wangi* is near to die',

'He died last year'! I cry in vain,
It seems he can do it again and again.

Never again that I should hear –
'Mama *wangi* is ill, I fear,
*Simu kuja* and I must go
Off to Hoima – or far Toro.

The Western Province appears to be
A most unhealthy locality,
Parents and friends die off in scores,
And I'm left alone with the household chores!

Masaka was reckoned to be a healthy station in that it was slightly cooler than Entebbe or Kampala and the mornings and evenings were pleasantly fresh. Like most stations it was perched on a hill, a custom reflecting an early theory that malaria was, quite literally, caused by the unhealthy miasma generated in low-lying marshy areas. Surrounding us as far as the eye could see were flourishing native *shamba*s, for it was a very fertile locality and specially suited to the cultivation of a plantain known as *matoki*, which formed the staple diet of the Baganda. This banana also provided the basis for a potent brew called *mwengi*, which we were soon to find was much favoured by our cook.

The station consisted of a small *duka* where the Indians and Goans lived and worked, while the Europeans, a dozen of us at most and all officials or wives of officials, were housed in a handful of bungalows close to the district commissioner's office, which was known as the *boma* – a term that originally meant an enclosure of thorns intended to keep out enemies or wild animals.

Although there were so few of us, the formalities were not forgotten. A few days after our arrival the district commissioner's wife, duly hatted and with visiting cards at the ready, called on me and explained that she had delayed visiting us until she saw that our curtains were up. In due course, naturally, I had to return the call.

As with all upcountry hospitals, the one at Masaka was about half a mile from the *boma* and was purely for the African population. My husband was kept busy dealing with their medical and minor surgical needs and looking after the outlying dispensaries. As these were within easy reach of the station by car there was no real need for safari. To some extent this was unfortunate from my point of view, for there were to be no further opportunities to go on a safari for several years and by that time we had six children so could not really take to the road *en famille*. The older generation spoke nostalgically of safaris in the days before cars, claiming that being on foot gave them better opportunities to get to know the people and their problems at grass-roots level. No doubt there was a good deal of truth in this, but on the other hand the improved communications meant that the various officials could get around their district more quickly and more frequently, and could be more easily available if any emergency cropped up.

I believe I was supposed to have absorbed the art of housekeeping from my mother, but as I have already said she seemed to have a knack for running her household by remote control and I had little idea of the mechanics of household management. I can remember compiling my first shopping list with the assistance of our head boy, Yohana, and the cook, Mateo, and being appalled at the number of items that seemed to be needed to keep us ticking over.

These two worthies, Yohana and Mateo, were just the mere nucleus of our domestic staff, which in no time at all totalled seven. If that sounds like a lot of people to see to the needs of my husband and myself, I can only say that it followed the normal scale. The combined efforts of all seven probably amounted to those of the cook, general char and jobbing gardener we would then have employed in England.

By far the most hard-working member of our staff – and of other people's – was the kitchen boy (*toto jikoni*). In addition to chopping wood for the Dover stove and producing tins of bath water on demand, he probably did a large part of the cooking and paid the cook a proportion of his wages for the privilege of doing so, for every self-respecting *toto jikoni* aspired to the dizzy height of becoming an *mpishi* (cook). Unlike the pantry *toto*, who enjoyed the refinements of an enamel bowl and blue-mottled soap when washing the crockery, the *toto jikoni* made efficient use of ash as a scouring agent for his pots and pans, which were then put out to dry in the sun on a sort of raised platform, which he constructed from branches broken off trees. It was important to keep an eye on the uprights of this platform, for unless there were obvious signs of growth the chances were that termites – commonly though incorrectly known as white ants – were busy with their destructive work down below. For a similar reason the *dhobi* had to keep a sharp eye on his clothes props, for negligence could mean the collapse of the day's washing – all of which would have to be done again.

These 'white ants' made ceaseless attempts to get into houses and were swift and adept at building ramps of earth over the concrete foundations from which to launch their offensives. Given half a chance, they made short work of wooden articles and would demolish any garments and paper left lying about. On the credit side they were excellent scavengers, though there was very much less litter in those pre-packaging days. Indeed, I sometimes think they could play a useful role in modern, litter-strewn Britain! They also had their uses when the auditor paid his dreaded annual visit to inspect government premises, for the absence of certain items of equipment could unanswerably be laid at their door. On one occasion it was even suggested that they had consumed an iron bedstead, but this proved too much for the auditor – let alone the white ants – to swallow.

The furniture the government issued was all made to standard designs from a beautiful but extremely heavy wood called *mvuli*. It was quite adequate for the bedrooms and dining room, but for the sitting room one had to rely much more on one's individual possessions and taste. We had acquired a few easy chairs and I had brought some cretonne out from England for loose covers. But, to my dismay, there was no *fundi* who could do that sort of work in Masaka, so I had to turn to and do my very inexpert best.

By far the most important piece of equipment in every colonial household, in Africa at least, was the Dover stove on which a succession of African cooks performed major miracles, including my mother's Tom in Nyasaland at the turn of the century. These stoves, which were rather baleful looking black objects perched incongruously on cabriole legs, had an insatiable appetite for *kuni* (firewood). The *mpishi* and his *toto* would work happily in a haze of smoke as the *memsahib* fought a losing battle to have the wood cut to short lengths that could be enclosed in the firebox. It was of course far less trouble to use long stakes that were gradually pushed in and I have to admit that the food was rarely tainted with smoke. Furthermore, the simple process of adding or subtracting *kuni* easily adjusted the oven temperature to hot or cool as the *memsahib*'s cake-making recipe required.

Another vital piece of equipment was the meat safe. This stood in the coolest corner of the back veranda with its legs immersed in tins of water and paraffin to foil the sugar ants, which needed only the slenderest 'bridge' to gain a foothold, and the would-be breeding mosquitoes. Though the sugar ants – as their name implies – had a preference for any sort of sweetmeat, no food was safe from their attentions and I once saw a large ham looking as if it were covered by a quivering black crust.

Out of doors it was important to look out for safari ants as they relentlessly travelled along in a black, rope-like formation; all was well if their progress was undisturbed, but if inadvertently interfered with they were quick to retaliate with needle sharp bites to all the least accessible parts of one's anatomy. There were horror stories about people on safari being mercilessly attacked in their sleep for no better reason than that they had innocently pitched their camp on the safari ants' intended route.

*Dudu*s (insects) of one sort or another constantly pre-occupied all housewives in Africa and a great deal of time and energy were spent trying to keep them at bay. Far more objectionable than the ants were the cockroaches – large, shiny, whiskered creatures against which we fought an endless and mainly unavailing war. Lacking modern insecticides we tried all sorts of methods of extermination, including one that involved filling shallow containers, like bottle tops, with water and a mixture of sugar and borax respectively; the creatures would eat the one, drink the other and solidify inside. This form of Chinese torture produced a number of corpses, but there were never-ending replacements from eggs laid in all sorts of inaccessible cracks and crannies.

Moths too were a constant threat; they had an uncanny ability to penetrate our so-called mothproof trunks in which our leave-going clothes were kept, and they seemed positively to enjoy mothballs. There were no man-made fabrics or polythene storage bags in those days, so unless a careful watch were kept our precious woollies could be reduced to a sort of broderie anglaise.

The most dreaded *dudu* of all was the mosquito, or rather the malaria-bearing female *anopheles*, a bite from which was almost invariably followed by a 'go' of fever ten days later. Before sundown every evening the house had to be 'flitted' as thoroughly as possible with a pyrethrum concoction in a small and rather ineffective hand pump, and every effort was made to see that the wire screens were kept closed. At night, of course, we slept within the stuffy safety of mosquito nets.

Much reliance was placed on blue-mottled soap, Vim and Jeyes fluid. Every day the cement floors would be scrubbed with water to which a dollop of Jeyes had been added. This was of course in the cause of general hygiene, but also in the hope of keeping down the jigger flea, which thrived in dust and had a delightful habit of laying its eggs in the human toe. A very itchy toe was a sign of trouble and then the tiny sac that contained the eggs had to be removed intact with a fine needle if a nasty septic toe were to be avoided.

Cement floors look very much more attractive than they sound, for when darkened by a solution of potassium permanganate they make an attractive background for the few rugs or mats that were all that was needed by way of floor coverings. Our houseboys greatly enjoyed polishing these floors by sliding around in 'slippers' made of felt or sheepskin, but their enthusiasm had to be restrained because the surface quickly became dangerously slippery.

Since for our water supply we relied entirely on the water that drained off our corrugated-iron roofs into cement tanks that filled up during the rainy season, water shortages were a great preoccupation. After several dry weeks it would be wonderful to hear the sound of a tropical downpour and the smell of the rain-soaked earth was almost intoxicatingly delectable. The first shower of rain, however, would wash a thick layer of red dust off the roof and into the tanks, so most of the water had to be drained away, which seemed almost like a sacrilege. Then one of the servants, usually the cook for some unknown reason, would climb into each tank through a trapdoor and give it a thorough scrubbing, so that it would be ready for the next cloudburst. Inevitably, it was either a feast or a fast, with water in abundance during the wet season and the need to economize severely at other times – and without much cooperation from our servants who were quite improvident in this respect.

Soap was bought in bars, which were then stacked in a lattice formation so that they would get as hard as possible and thus more economical in use. Each 'boy' would receive one piece of the blue-mottled variety each week with which to wash himself and his garments. The superior yellow soap was officially reserved for our laundry, though it was well known that the *dhobi* regarded quite a generous proportion of it as his rightful perk. The *dhobi* was a wonder worker; with the most primitive equipment he handled all the household laundry, including the damask table linen, which was in daily use, and the *bwana*'s evening shirts and collars, which were also in daily use. Although these had to be carefully starched and then pressed with a charcoal-filled box iron that was prone to emit sparks, there was rarely any cause to complain about his handiwork.

Our lighting was by oil lamps, which gave off a soft and attractive light but not a very good one for reading or sewing; they also needed a lot of maintenance in the form of filling, wick trimming and chimney polishing. A fairly new development at that time was the Aladdin lamp, which had an incandescent mantle and gave off a much better light. Later this was superseded by pressure lamps, which were vastly superior but needed careful management in that the methylated spirits with which they were lit would flare up in an alarming manner. For general use, the safari lantern was by far the most reliable and was much the safest to use in the bedroom with its inflammable mosquito nets.

One slight domestic improvement came when bucket latrines were tacked onto the back of the house so that one no longer had to resort to a hut in the garden. But we relied heavily on the ministrations of a nocturnal gang with whose noisome conveyance, known as the Midnight Express, one sometimes had embarrassing encounters. On one occasion a friend of ours had car trouble late at night and appealed to the gang to give him a helpful shove, only to be told 'No, no! We are government officials!' These worthies were known as Mackenzies, for this had been the name of the junior official who had originally been given the doubtful pleasure of organizing this invaluable service. Rest camps were always provided with pit latrines comprised of a deep hole over which a thunderbox stood on a platform of branches roughly plastered with earth. Unfortunately, this construction was not immune from the attentions of white ants, as one new and very dapper young cadet found to his cost! Thereafter he always insisted on the local headman conducting a thorough personal inspection before entering the holy of holies himself.

It must be difficult for anyone below middle age to imagine life without a fridge, particularly in the tropics, but here again we took the inconvenience for granted. Inevitably it meant that butter was soft and oily and meat, which had to be killed, cooked and eaten on the same day, bore a strong resemblance to shoe leather. Milk, a dubious commodity at best, had to be boiled the moment it arrived and again in the evening if it were to be kept overnight. Water too had to be boiled and it was often necessary to filter it as well. Vegetables were plentiful though rather insipid, but we had excellent fruit: pineapples, papaws, granadillas and bananas were particularly good, but for some reason oranges never seemed to ripen properly and were used chiefly for juice with a good deal of sweetening. Kenyan dairy products were excellent and very reasonably priced, with butter for instance the equivalent of only 7½ pence a pound. In Masaka we were fortunate in having fresh fish, which came from a little lake called Nabugabo (of which more later). All fish was known as *ngege*, but the one in general use was *tilapia*, which could be prepared in a number of very palatable ways. The fruit and vegetables in the market would be arranged in little piles on squares of banana leaf, with each pile costing ten cents. Since there were 100 cents to a shilling, the cost of living was very low indeed, at least with respect to local produce. Imported goods, though, were very expensive by the standards of those times.

Another indication of the low cost of living is that our

servants' monthly wages amounted to only 160 shillings, the equivalent of £8 – and they provided their own food. Of course there was a little filching of such things as tea and sugar, but as long as it was kept within reasonable bounds one learnt to turn a blind eye. The storeroom was kept locked and, in theory at least, only opened once a day, but the key had a way of getting mislaid. By this time my husband's salary had reached £880 per annum, but even so the modest wage bill and monthly repayments on the car made quite a dent, as did the compulsory contributions to the Widows and Orphans Pension Scheme. We also made a small but generally adequate provision for our next leave by remitting £10 each month to our bank in England. In all I should think we were left with about £35 a month to cover food and general expenses – a very small sum by modern standards, but we knew where we were with it as the cost of living never varied from one year to the next.

Looking back I find it hard to imagine how I occupied my days, but I certainly thought I was very busy with house-keeping after a fashion, coping with my daunting chair covers and making garments for our first baby, which was expected shortly. In fact my needlework was quite an achievement because I had hitherto shown little liking or aptitude for that sort of activity.

In the larger centres – Kampala, Entebbe and Jinja – there were native, European and Asian hospitals and everyone took the need for such distinctions for granted; after all, we thought, the Africans' tastes and standards were still very primitive, while the Asians and Europeans differed consider-ably from each other in terms of diet and social customs.

Great efforts were being made to reduce infant mortality among the Africans by encouraging mothers to have their babies in hospital, and in Masaka this encouragement took the form of a little dress the hospital sewing boy produced for each newcomer. These garments were greatly prized and the maternity section was always full to overflowing. I enjoyed visiting these mothers and their babies, which must surely be the most attractive of human young, when I accompanied my husband on his evening round. I think the Asian women had their babies in their homes, with the assistance of assorted relatives and friends, though I can remember Arthur being called on to attend to some of them. On one occasion his patient was the postmaster's wife and he found all the older children bedded down for the night on the post office counter. There were absolutely no facilities for having European babies upcountry – perhaps because we were less resourceful or lacked helpful relatives and friends – so we decided that our baby should be born in the Entebbe European hospital. My parents were still living in Entebbe, though they were shortly due to move to Kampala where the new high court was nearing completion. So, about ten days before my expected date of delivery, my husband took me to stay with them so as to be conveniently poised for the event.

Having a baby was much more of a performance in those days than it is now. Had I been in England (or Ireland) the birth would probably have taken place at home, with a 'monthly' nurse to wait hand and foot on me and the infant, and a nanny or at least a nursery maid to take over when she departed. As it is, I spent a full fortnight in hospital after the birth of our son, Michael, and during the first week I never put a toe out of bed and was visited only by my husband and parents. During the second week I was allowed up for gradually lengthening periods, was instructed in the art of bathing the baby and was complacently available to all and sundry who came bearing gifts and congratulations. All this fuss certainly made me feel very important but I am sure there was a psychological disadvantage in being isolated so long from the domestic scene.

Meanwhile, an *ayah* (nursemaid) was engaged to return with me to Masaka and I was thereby relieved of all the chores but none of the responsibility. Although the women employed as *ayah*s were pleasant and willing, with so little education available to girls at that time, they needed a great deal of supervision with regard to their own hygiene, quite apart from that of their small charges. Over the years a sort of *corps d'élite* of *ayah*s emerged as the result of much patient training on the part of a succession of *memsahib*s, but they were always at their best with very young children and it was rare to find one who could provide the discipline or stimulation needed once the toddler stage was left behind.

Perhaps this is an appropriate point at which to describe what was then the normal routine for European children in Uganda. Through a general fear of sunstroke they were incarcerated indoors between 8.30 a.m. and 4 p.m.; if by any chance they had to emerge between those hours they would wear *topi*s or double Terais and even spine pads, in extreme cases, for protection. Perhaps because of his childhood in British Guiana, my husband felt that these precautions were excessive. So we were to cause some alarm when we allowed our children to play outdoors at will wearing sunsuits, which must have been the first to be seen in the country, and hats made of a single layer of felt or even cotton. Perhaps we were pioneers in this small way, for when no ill effects were noted other families followed suit and the children certainly seemed to have benefited.

Also at this stage, and with a view to avoiding what might seem like a boringly repetitive theme, I must explain that by the end of 1938 our family numbered seven and that additions during and after the war eventually brought the grand total to ten.

In 1930, however, in blissful ignorance of the formidable responsibilities that lay ahead, I seemed very fully occupied in caring for Michael in accordance with the wise if over rigid edicts of Truby King, the nursery oracle of that era. Admittedly, I was an anxious mother, but in fairness it must be said that with respect to health there was quite a lot to be anxious about. Malaria was still prevalent and though adults took regular 'goes' as an inevitable fact of tropical life, it was a different matter for young children and the slightest rise in temperature had to be taken seriously. The malarial parasite does not always show up in a blood slide and it was too risky to 'wait and see', so many a painful injection of quinine was given for what later turned out to be a minor childhood upset. As in Nyasaland 20 years earlier, dysentery also posed a threat, and a very insidious one; mosquitoes at least made one aware of their presence but without the safeguards of waterborne sanitation and refrigeration the dreaded bacillus sometimes got through our defences.

Sleeping sickness had been rife in some parts of Uganda, but it had largely been brought under control by moving the population away from tsetse fly breeding places like the Sese Islands, and destroying the vegetation in which they throve. I only knew of two Europeans who contracted the disease and one of them was our district commissioner in Masaka, Tuppence Harvey. Both cases were technically 'cured', but poor Tuppence was apt to nod off in a way that was embarrassing for all concerned.

Most people played golf or tennis for a couple of hours after tea and afterwards there would be a certain amount of getting together in each other's houses for 'sundowners'. Although there were so few of us in Masaka, as I mentioned earlier, our social lives revolved largely around formal five-course dinner parties, which started and finished respectively with what were called first and second toasties. The first of these was almost invariably an elaborately stuffed egg – our cook was a real artist in this respect – perched on a round of buttered bread, while the second was something hot like cheese straws or devils-on-horseback. Several years later, when sundowner parties became fashionable, the canapés served at them were referred to as 'toasties' – and they still are in former East African circles.

My first dinner guests were unexpected and, in an effort

to cheer up the menu, I nearly poisoned them! I told the cook to put some sherry in the soup and handed him a bottle, about a quarter full, which had been among various bits and pieces of groceries given to me by my sister-in-law before she and my brother went on leave. As we sat down to dinner there was a strong smell of furniture polish, which, I presumed, had been over liberally applied to the table. It was only with the first mouthful of soup that I realized that this was where the smell – to say nothing of the taste – was coming from. I then remembered to my horror that my sister-in-law had mentioned that the bottle contained home-made furniture polish in a compound of turpentine, linseed oil and vinegar. Happily, very little had been swallowed and no harm was done, but one of our guests was a hypo-chondriac and he was convinced that he would never see daylight again and henceforth always treated meals in our household with the greatest suspicion.

The sports facilities in Masaka amounted to one tennis court and a very rudimentary golf course. At weekends we sometimes went to Lake Nabugabo, about 12 miles away, for a swim. This little lake was separated from Victoria by a narrow strip of marshy ground, but for some unknown reason it was free of crocodiles, although it was to lose its immunity with startling suddenness some years later.

Our stay in Masaka was destined to be a short one for, after about eight months, my husband was detailed to do a leprosy survey of Buganda and was then posted to Mulago where we remained until 1937.

*Mulago/Kampala: 1931–37*
Although Entebbe resembled a village in appearance, the similarity ended there for it was over endowed with lords of the manor in the persons of the directors of the various departments. In Kampala we were all more or less on a level – give or take a few years of 'seniority' – so, although the European population was far larger than in Entebbe, we all

seemed to know each other as one does in the pleasant informality of a village. Nonetheless, we continued to invite each other to dinner parties and dinner jackets and somewhat downgraded evening dresses were regularly worn, even in the home circle.

As in Entebbe, our social highlight was a monthly dance at the club, which had a newly constructed ballroom with the unique distinction of a wooden floor, which was a lot easier on one's feet than the usual cement. It also boasted a stage, which was a great asset to local amateur performers among whom I later came to be numbered. In general, the clubs were all male strongholds and women were only grudgingly given access to a veranda referred to as the 'boat deck' and to the library. Apart from a little home-grown music and occasional theatricals, we had absolutely no cultural outlets other than one cinema, which functioned, more or less, with the aid of a paraffin-powered generator. Games were played with great enthusiasm for a couple of hours after *saa kumi* – literally 10 p.m. by African reckoning but 4 p.m. 'government' time. This matter of time could be rather confusing because the Africans preferred to keep 'God's time', which meant that 7 a.m. or thereabouts was referred to as *saa moja* (1 a.m.) and on dark wet mornings the Almighty tended, understandably, to have a lie-in.

Kampala was very much a garden city with the emphasis on the 'garden', for even the smallest bungalow was set in a large tree-shaded compound. Most English flowers flourished alongside the more exotic ones and among a variety of colourful shrubs and creepers the purple bougainvillaea predominated. This attractive scene was rather marred by our corrugated iron roofs, which had to remain unpainted because even in this relative hub of civilization we still relied on them as catchments for our water supply.

The main residential quarter was on the upper slopes of Nakasero Hill with government offices below. Beneath them came Kampala Road with its straggle of *duka*s plus a few slightly more pretentious shops, banks and commercial agencies; and at a lower level still the Indians lived and worked in a warren of little streets.

Over the years Kampala's suburban sprawl spread to several neighbouring hillsides, but the only government outposts in the early 1930s were Makerere College and Mulago Hospital. The Buganda government's headquarters were sited on a hill called Mengo, close to the Kabaka's palace, and the Anglican and Catholic cathedrals, churches, schools and hospitals topped yet more hills.

Our house at Mulago was brand new in the Public Works Department's latest style. It had enclosed verandas at back and front, good-sized sitting and dining rooms, but only one bedroom with a dressing room off it. We also had a small study, which had to serve as a spare room, but it was very inconveniently placed for our toilet facilities, which were as basic as ever.

Our nearest neighbour was the married woman doctor already mentioned, but her house, also a new one, had twice as much accommodation as ours (which was in keeping with her *katibwa*) even though she merely camped in it during the week and took herself off to her husband's equally roomy bungalow in Entebbe at the weekends.

Housing was allocated strictly according to seniority and the higher up the scale one went the more bedrooms one could hope to have, even though one's need for family accommodation was by then probably at an end. The government still insisted that European children could not be kept in the tropics after the age of seven and thereby saved itself the trouble of providing even the most rudimentary schooling. Over the border in Kenya, which was generally regarded as healthier than Uganda, Loreto Convent had been established since 1921 and junior schools were gradually opening up in the Highlands. But no such efforts had been made in Uganda and it was to take the Second World

War, when children could not possibly be sent overseas, to rouse the Uganda government in this respect. Meanwhile, the thought of parting with our children hung over us and other parents. But in that we would be able to send them to Kenya for their early schooling we knew that we would be more fortunate than earlier generations.

With the new high court completed – the first double-storey building to come off the government architect's drawing board – my parents had, perforce, to move to Kampala. Though they disliked the upheaval greatly, it was compensated for to some extent by the enlargement of an already roomy bungalow to provide them with a colonial style stately home. I was to see this house through varying fortunes in the years to come. After the war, when a more modern residence was built for the chief justice, it was converted into flats and in 1954 I was actively involved in the alterations and extensions that turned it into the Uganda (Interracial) Club. In the 1930s, however, its large rooms and shady verandas certainly contributed to the *katibwa* of my father and his successors.

About this time – perhaps so as not to be outdone by the legal department's flight of fancy – Uganda's only private architect was engaged to draw up plans for an up-to-date palace for the Kabaka. This was also meant to be a double-storey building but the architect, who understandably had little experience in this respect, merely designed two bungalows, one to be placed on top of the other. He then found that the staircase had to be rather awkwardly contrived – to the detriment of the one and only bathroom, which ended up with an embarrassing number of doors.

Meanwhile, my brother had transferred from the administration to the legal department and served first as registrar to the High Court and later as crown counsel. Thereafter, promotion took him to the Bahamas, Palestine and Hong Kong until eventually he came full circle with his return to Uganda as chief justice in 1952. This of course is a mere

8. The law courts, Kampala, Uganda. The original building, c.1930, dated from the period of Sir Charles Griffin's tenure as chief justice. The two end wings were added, successfully in keeping with the older part, when his son Sir John Griffin was chief justice, early 1950s.

skeleton of my brother's career, but there is a fuller account given by his daughter Mary later in the book.

In the early 1930s the staff at Mulago numbered half a dozen doctors and a similar number of 'sisters', as all European nurses were called, and under them were African orderlies and ward maids. Doctors, who had to be jacks of all trades, dealt with medical and surgical problems as they arose and also lectured in the newly formed medical school. In addition to his normal duties, Arthur was understudying the medical superintendent, Dr Owen, in his secondary capacity as 'eye doctor' – the first specialist to be recognized by the princely allowance of £100 per annum. The superintendent was exempt from night duty but the others took their turn and our sleep was often disturbed by the arrival of an orderly with a hurricane lamp announcing some emergency or other. That same hurricane lamp provided the light for whatever treatment or surgery was indicated and instruments were sterilized on a primus stove. Conditions were indeed primitive but the doctors were keen and mostly young and brought great enthusiasm to their varied tasks.

By 1931, Mulago had developed considerably from the small dispensary Major Keane had started. Even so it still consisted mainly of a group of one-storey wards connected by concrete passages, while the outpatient clinic tended to be a free-for-all. During our early days at Mulago we watched the construction of a new outpatient clinic with much interest, for it represented a great leap forward in terms of East African medical facilities. With its completion, it became easier to channel the patients according to their particular needs and the whole process became much more streamlined. Treatment in the fields of both medicine and surgery was gradually becoming more sophisticated. Though a general surgeon, Alan Mowat, was appointed about that time, it was only after the war, some 15 years later, that specialities came to be regarded as appointments in their own right, rather than sidelines to be fitted in along with the general duties of a medical officer. There had been no dramatic advances in terms of medication. With bacillary dysentery, for instance, castor oil was still the sovereign remedy, as I found to my cost when I went down with a bad attack just six weeks before our second baby, Peter, was due. There was of course a danger that the treatment would cause premature labour, but fortunately that did not happen. Then, when I was in hospital having safely produced our second son, Michael, who was barely 14 months old, contracted malaria and had to be subjected to a horribly painful quinine injection – there was simply no alternative when quinine could not be taken orally.

There was no social intermingling of the races then and little thought about its desirability until after the Second

World War, by which time educational advances had made the process easier. To a casual observer the Africans were polite and amiable to an almost obsequious degree, but to my regret they were, and perhaps remain, an enigmatic people with whom I had difficulty making real contact. Perhaps it was because, as with Africa itself, I feel the lack of a shared historical and cultural background.

Certainly, in the 1930s there was little sign of the astonishing changes that the next quarter century was to bring, and if independence were thought of at all it was in terms of the dim and distant future.

I recall two special events in 1931. The first was no less than a plague of locusts on a truly biblical scale. We had no warnings of the impending invasion and did not at first grasp the significance of a small and distant cloud until it bore down on us with alarming speed and ever-increasing density as the air became thick with a myriad of whirring bodies. We could do nothing but retreat into our houses and ensure that every door and window was firmly closed. For several hours it was impossible even to see through the windows. As the swarm continued on its way we looked out on the desolation it had left in its wake: not a blade of grass or leaf had been spared. We might have been in the middle of a desert had the locusts not shunned the flowers, which were left stark and incongruous on their naked stems. This was bad enough, but far more serious was the realization that vegetation and grazing had been destroyed over a large area and there was virtually no fresh food to be had. Prematurely, we congratulated ourselves on a productive hen run, only to find that the birds had gorged on the locusts and their eggs had a fishy flavour and were quite inedible.

The African countryside has great recuperative powers and greenery was gradually reappearing when we woke one morning to find the ground covered by a heaving, slithery mass of creatures that looked rather like brownish sardines.

The locusts had laid their eggs before moving on and these were the newly hatched 'hoppers'. Once more our hens made the most of their opportunities, but fortunately there was insufficient vegetation to sustain the fledglings and, before they in turn reached the egg-laying stage, they had flown on to pastures new.

The second event, which came towards the end of the year, was of a very different order and provided us with our first experience of the impact of the 'slump' that was affecting Western countries with growing severity. It took the form of an ordinance giving advance notice of a levy of between 5 and 7½ per cent to be raised on all salaries. Although in modern circumstances it seems absurd that such a small sum should have caused so much indignation, in those days even £40 was more than any of us could afford to part with lightly. The ordinance was not enforced until 1933 and it operated, I believe, for three years. With only about 560 officials in the country, however, it is hard to imagine that our unwilling contributions made any real difference to the national emergency.

Another victim of the slump, though on a more serious scale, was Michael Moses whose business interests were severely affected. At the time we knew little about his anxieties because he kept them to himself, but years later, when a timely association with tin mining in Rwanda-Urundi had more than retrieved his fortunes, he told me that for years all his properties had been heavily mortgaged.

By the time we went on leave in April 1932 the railway had reached Kampala, so we no longer had to make the lake crossing to Kisumu. It was on arrival in England that we, personally, were seriously affected by the slump. My husband had applied for an extension of leave in order to qualify for the DOMS (Diploma of Ophthalmic Medicine and Surgery, now known simply as the DO), which would normally have been granted on full pay. So it was a shock to learn that, although the additional leave was confirmed, it would be on half pay and that all fees would be at our personal expense. This meant that for the final three months of our time in England we would have to get by on at most £35 a month. Even in those days this was insufficient to cover the living costs of a family of five – our third child, Margaret, having been born in the summer. In that era loans and mortgages were serious matters and it was with great trepidation that we approached our bank manager with a request for a loan of £100, which, amazing though it now seems, sufficed to tide us over this difficult period.

When we returned to Uganda in February 1933 with the diploma safely secured, it was daunting to know that we were starting our new tour in the 'red' and we were thankful indeed when the debt was fully repaid several months later. A further anxiety was that at first it seemed that the coveted £100 per annum of which my husband had been assured once he got the diploma – his predecessor in the field had retired – would not be forthcoming. A new director of medical services who did not hold with such things had taken over and it was only after much deliberation that he grudgingly agreed to honour his predecessor's promise.

Mulago's new medical superintendent Dr J. P. Mitchell, always known as JP, was an urbane Scot and bon viveur. He and his wife Loui had married late and had no children, but they certainly had a very parental attitude towards the Mulago staff. Loui was a housewife in the best Scottish tradition, so one could always count on excellent food when invited to their house, though inevitably the return match was a bit of a strain for a tiro like myself. It was Loui who introduced me to the pressure cooker, which worked wonders with our tropical meat, and she also taught me to make oatcakes – on my twenty-first birthday of all days!

There was one rather older couple that tended to keep themselves to themselves. They had previously been with the Church Missionary Society and we wondered why they had left what must have been a more congenial environment. However, the nickname he had acquired during those days – in translation 'the knife slipped on me' – may have provided a clue, and I rather think that his surgical opportunities were kept to a minimum at Mulago. His wife had a nasty shock one day when she discovered that her cook, whom she had taken a lot of trouble to train and who was supposed to be a good Christian, had three wives. She told him sternly that he would have to part with two of them, but the culprit declined, maintaining that he was equally attached to all three. With Christian principles at stake on the one hand and having no wish to lose a good cook on the other, this posed quite a problem. Happily, the British genius for compromise came to her aid and he was informed that henceforth two wives would be in order.

Living in such a purely medical enclave could have been rather claustrophobic, but in general it worked out happily with the husbands cooperating in their professional lives and the wives and children mutually companionable. With the big city only a short distance away, most people took off after tea to enjoy a couple of hours on its tennis courts or on the golf course, which at that time ran alongside the residential area on Nakasero Hill.

Once we had re-established our financial equilibrium we felt justified in purchasing an Electrolux oil-burning fridge, though the outlay of £35 nearly put us back in the red. This seemed like the last word in luxury and it made a great difference to our life, though it was not entirely reliable and sometimes defrosted, leaving the cabinet awash and its contents in a parlous state. The first time this happened I hastily rang up the supplier and was astonished to be told to turn the fridge upside down and give it a good shake. This seemed harsh treatment to mete out to our new toy, but it had the desired effect of shifting the airlock that had caused the trouble. We frequently had to resort to this procedure but never had to go as far as some friends who used to put

9. Retirement of Sir Charles Griffin as chief justice, Uganda, outside law courts, Kampala. John Bowes Griffin is on the far left, middle row, 1932.

their fridge in the back of a safari car and give it a bumpy ride.

In 1932 my father decided to retire – a decision that filled my mother with dismay, for she was happy with the familiar pattern of her East African life, loved her African servants dearly and dreaded the uncertainties of the English climate and domestic scene. My father was then only 56, which seems young for retirement by modern standards. But after 31 years spent mostly in the tropics he felt he had had enough of the colonial service and, although bridge and armchair cricket were his only hobbies, he greatly looked forward to the end of his working life.

My father's retirement coincided roughly with the intro-duction of a scheme that allowed one to commute a quarter of one's pension in exchange for a lump sum with which to purchase a house. After doing this, his annual pension came to £1200 and he was able to a buy a beautiful house in

Guernsey in the Channel Islands for £1800. Retiring colonial officials had big ideas in those days and the house was unnecessarily large and imposing. But, with an income augmented by investments to around £1600, they could afford three resident servants and looked forward to providing a base for their married children when they came on leave.

Not long after my parents' departure from Uganda the Sunderland flying boats started to make a regular appearance. We enjoyed driving down to Port Bell, about 12 miles from Kampala, to watch the arrival and departure of this modern miracle, which cut travelling time between East Africa and the United Kingdom from a month to three days. Of course, for passengers it was a prestige service and not for the likes of us. But at least our letters could wing their way and it was wonderful to be able to correspond and exchange news so much more quickly.

Our next leave came in 1935 and it was spent under the parental roof. However, although this was what they had been accustomed to in their youth, the 'servant problem' was rearing its head. Now with five children and a nanny, such a large influx was too much of a good thing and, grateful though we were for my parents' hospitality, we resolved that in future we would stand on our own feet.

Nowadays we are mercifully immune from servants and the problems they created, but up to the time of the Second World War they loomed very large in the life of the British housewife. It seems ironic that in my old age, with minimal domestic help, I am much less exhausted both mentally and physically by family invasions than my mother was with three servants to be catered for, humoured and supervised.

By 1936 Kampala had grown considerably and, although we still awaited the benefits of mains drainage, piped water and electricity, the roads seemed to be in a perpetual state of being dug up in the cause of one or the other, so we lived in hope. Shopping facilities had hardly improved at all, so everyone stocked up when they went on leave with shoes and 'better' garments, and relied on home dressmaking or on Indian or Goan tailors for everyday frocks and suits, which wore out rapidly in the strong sunlight.

The cinema had not greatly improved, but some people had radios – or wirelesses as they were called – and we were very proud of the Pye battery set we acquired in 1936. With English papers still taking a month or more to arrive, it was wonderful to be kept up to date with world events, however crackly they sounded. Several friends came in to hear Edward VIII's abdication speech, which seemed to be a world-shattering event at the time. In due course there was an elaborate fireworks display in Kampala to celebrate the coronation of George VI and Queen Elizabeth. Since this took place at the Nakivubo football ground, in a rather low-lying area where one was likely to pick up malaria, Michael and Peter, whom we felt should witness this historic occasion, were clad in pyjamas, raincoats and gumboots in the hope of foiling the mosquitoes and, happily, the precautions were successful.

There had been no significant reduction in the incidence of malaria, but with most people owning fridges one heard less about bacillary dysentery. The government, however, still clung to the theory that white children could not survive in Uganda after the age of seven, so the only education available was a small nursery school run by an admirable lady in a pokey little bungalow known as the 'Black Hole of Calcutta'. This was attended by our eldest son Michael, and in due course by his junior Peter; then Michael was sent off to a boarding school at Turi in the Kenya Highlands.

*Fort Portal: 1938–39*
Like the proverbial private with a field marshal's baton in his rucksack, some young men seemed destined from the start of their colonial career to go to the top. But in general promotion depended far more on length of service than on

individual merit or qualifications. So, in 1937, when our sixth child was a few months old, we underwent a change of scene and status. Arthur became a senior medical officer and was posted to Fort Portal in the Western Province, which I had visited twice in my 'flapper' days. Inevitably, it meant that ophthalmology would have to be put in abeyance (and everyone would have to do without this service) as the new job was mainly administrative and would entail a lot of safari. Financially, of course, it was a step up, which we were in no position to refuse. I believe my husband's salary then rose to £1000 – no small sum in those days – but he had to forfeit the non-pensionable ophthalmic allowance.

Our new home turned out to be a very ancient bungalow that looked even more like a meat safe than most; it consisted of a string of four dark rooms, completely enclosed in wired-in verandas, the end sections of which we used as extra bedroom accommodation. We had been warned that the proximity of the Ruwenzori mountains tended to have a depressing effect and it was true that this rather uninteresting range did seem to loom over us; only during the rainy season were we rewarded, morning and evening, with dazzling views of the snowy Mountains of the Moon. Another depressing factor was that the rains, which were particularly heavy in that area, were at their most torrential in the afternoons when one wanted to be out of doors.

Fort Portal's European population numbered only about half a dozen officials, mostly married but with children already being educated in England, so it was just as well our family had plenty of built-in companionship. Our houses were grouped around the *boma*, which in turn was surrounded by a moat. Most people, including Arthur, spent at least one-third of each month on safari, touring their district or province. I was thus often in a rather lonely situation, for of course we were far too numerous to join my husband. It is perhaps worth noting that in those peaceful and law-abiding days it occurred to no one – least of all me – that my frequently solitary state might be any cause for anxiety.

Stations had a way of being either 'happy' or the reverse, depending on how the constituent members hit it off with one another and, on the whole, we were fortunate in Fort Portal. We were certainly free from the feuds that sometimes beset small communities and generally arise because a slight or grievance – real or imaginary – is blown up out of all proportion. One very long-lasting feud arose (though not in Fort Portal) because a resourceful head boy, realizing he was short of a coffee cup for the evening's dinner party, borrowed one from a neighbour's head boy. Unfortunately, the latter's employers were among the guests and they took great umbrage at the appearance of their familiar crockery.

Toro was almost unique in Uganda in having a group of settlers, known as 'planters'. Coffee had long been their mainstay but tea had recently been introduced and one of the more prosperous members of the group had built a factory in which to process it. Some planters had wives and families and led ordered lives, but a few wild men among them had unusual domestic arrangements. I think they rather enjoyed being regarded as 'characters' and I admired the ingenuity of one who solved his plumbing problems by building his house and latrine over a stream so that he had a constant supply of water at one end and mains drainage at the other. Presumably, there were no near neighbours downstream to be inconvenienced by his arrangement.

Our only social contact with Africans in Toro was when the *Omukama* (ruler of Toro district), generally known as George of Toro, invited us to tea. His residence, which consisted of a group of huts of various sizes, was on top of a conical hill about a mile from the *boma*. George was an enormous man. Size seemed to run in his family because he was surrounded by a number of Amazonian women whom, I was told, were either his wives or his sisters.

I led a very circumscribed life and, apart from the interest and occupation my family provided, my physical and mental horizons were narrow indeed and I rarely got away from the station. So, when some friends came from Entebbe on local leave and suggested Peter and I join them for a day's outing over the Ruwenzori mountains to Bundabugio, I was delighted to accept. By this time I had an exceptionally reliable *ayah* and felt that she could safely be left to cope with the four little girls for a few hours.

Arthur's first safari to Bundabugio had of necessity to be on foot, for the spiralling, precipitous road we took was one of the Public Works Department's more recent achievements. Bundabugio was then – and I imagine still is – a primitive settlement. Its inhabitants, the Bakonjo, were nearly as small as pygmies and, with men and women alike having pot bellies and spindly legs, they seemed, at least to us, unattractive in face and form. They lived in flimsy beehive-like huts made of elephant grass and bamboo and when, several years later, I heard via the BBC that an earthquake had destroyed several 'buildings' in Bundabugio, I felt that the job of reconstruction would not pose too great a problem.

According to geologists, the Ruwenzori range is in the process of 'settling', which makes the area earthquake prone and minor quakes were a frequent occurrence. We did, however, experience one quite alarming quake when the ground beneath our feet seemed anything but stable and large cracks appeared in buildings and roads.

Fort Portal was regarded as a healthy station, chiefly because it was cooler than most, but it was to be the scene of the most serious illness our family was to experience. I had always had a particular dread of infantile paralysis – as poliomyelitis was then called – for I had seen a couple of tragic examples of the ravages this disease could cause. While no case had been recorded in Uganda, we occasionally saw Africans with disabilities that must have resulted from this or a similar illness. We had been in Fort Portal about eight months when the blow fell in no uncertain manner.

I had to go to Kampala to pick up Michael who was returning from Kenya by train for the holidays, so seized the opportunity to take our second daughter, Gemma, with me because she needed some minor treatment from our surgeon friend, Alan Mowat. He and his young wife, Wilmet, very kindly put us up and, while we were with them, she became ill and was taken to hospital with a painful but undiagnosed complaint. The day after our return to Fort Portal we received a telegram with the appalling news that Wilmet had died and that the cause of her death was still undiagnosed.

Just a week later when Gemma suffered very similar symptoms, Arthur was on safari and could not be reached. But the nursing sister, Eleanor Bolton, was a tower of strength then and throughout our weeks of anxiety.[2] On Arthur's return the following day he thought at first that meningitis was a possibility, but when tests ruled that out he quickly realized we had infantile paralysis on our hands.

At this late date I have no wish to relive those weeks of acute anxiety, but prefer rather to recall the kindness and concern of people of every race and creed and the providential circumstances that saved us – and others – from what could easily have been a major calamity. The first of these was that, with few children in the neighbourhood and none at all in the actual station, the virus did not spread beyond our own family. The second was that, although the children were very ill, not one developed the pulmonary symptoms that would have been fatal because there was not a single iron lung in the country at the time. Finally, I, though six months pregnant and thus particularly vulnerable, did not

2. Eleanor later married Jim Dakin who wrote the foreword to this book (editor).

succumb. Indeed, as convalescence followed its slow course, I realized I had actually reaped a benefit, for, having nursed my family through one of the worst possible illnesses, I became far less worried by the possibility of lesser ones.

In due course our seventh child, Jocelyn, was safely born. After the recent stresses and strains we were far too thankful to have a healthy, normal little girl to worry unduly about her being the fifth daughter in a row. A few days after her birth I was amused when my Scottish friend Loui Mitchell visited and presented me with a brooch of five graduated little white elephants. I thought it was a joke, but fortunately before I showed my amusement I realized she had not meant it that way – it was simply something with which to 'fasten the child's shawl'!

The four months before we went on leave were busy ones for me. Michael had been unable to return to school in Kenya following his illness, so I had to try to impart the three 'R's' to him and to his two immediate juniors, Peter and Margaret.

To avoid the rigours of winter we extended our tour and set off on leave in March 1939, taking the longer route around the Cape to give England a chance to warm up before our arrival. We spent several sweltering days at Beira while a cargo of copper destined for Germany was loaded onto our Union Castle ship; a French fellow passenger was moved to exclaim: 'Oh! You British! Don't you know you'll soon be getting all this back on your heads?'

☼ ☼ ☼ ☼ ☼

It seems appropriate at this point to include the memories of his childhood up to 1939 of my brother Peter (Arthur and Alice Boase's son) (editor).

☼ ☼ ☼ ☼ ☼

103

## An African childhood by Peter Boase

Dad was born in British Guiana, which is considered part of the Caribbean. On his birth certificate it says that his father is British and that his mother is a white native of St Lucia. He spent two-thirds of his working life as a government medical officer in Uganda, so that is where most of us were born. I suppose we could thus claim to be Afro-Caribbean.

Kampala, the commercial capital of Uganda, was a fairly primitive place in those days before the war. There was no electricity, mains water or sewerage and only about half a mile of tarmac road. Though I have no memory of it, there must have been a telephone system. Our water supply came from the rain of the frequent thunder storms being drained off the roof and stored in a couple of large tanks; and the servants transported it to wherever it was required in four-gallon kerosene cans. Bath water was heated on a wood-burning stove in the kitchen. All this fetching and carrying required a fair number of servants, but that was the way things were and we thought nothing of it.

Like Rome, Kampala was built on seven hills and one's social status decreed on which hill and how far up one lived. Europeans inhabited the upper reaches, Indians were halfway down and the Africans lived in the valleys. We initially lived on Mulago Hill, which was where the African hospital and medical facilities were. We didn't live quite at the top – that was reserved for the medical superintendent – but near enough to make a difference.

That hilltop featured in one of my earliest memories (I was three at the time). Dad had left his car parked in front of the bungalow on the steepest part of the hill – probably to help it start with a no doubt unreliable battery. My older brother Michael, then four years old, rounded up my sister Margaret, two, and me to practise some driving. We were all aboard when he let off the brake. I can still see Dad shouting and running after us as we took off and left the

104

road for the sheer hillside. *Mungu* (God) must have been watching over us because a well-placed gum tree soon brought us to a halt. The repair bill came to £30, which was money in those days, and Dad was not amused.

Cars figure in another of my early memories. Like all European children there, our nanny would take us for an early morning walk before breakfast. (We had an English nanny then, so we could not have been as poor as we had been led to believe.) Bobby, a fox terrier we were looking after for the medical superintendent and his wife who were on leave, would come with us. Bobby was a confirmed car chaser and I can still remember him barking like mad at the rear wheels of every passing car as he disappeared into the cloud of dust that rose from the dirt road. Then, one morning, when the dust subsided there was Bobby writhing in agony as he dragged himself off the road into the elephant grass. I pulled him out by his collar and Nanny carried him home. By midday he was cold and stiff and Juma, the *shamba* boy (notable for having six digits on his left hand) was digging his grave.

I suppose I must have been about four years old – we were still in the English nanny era – when one night an African wearing a striped nightshirt climbed into my bed and threw me out. There must have been quite a lot of disturbance leading up to this because Nanny was on hand to catch me. The man had escaped from the mental asylum just down the road, though I do not know how he got out and found his way into our house.

About this time, a Mrs Holmes started a nursery school in her bungalow across the valley on Nakasero Hill – though not very high up I should add – to which first Michael and then I were sent as we turned five. For me it was the end of an idyllic period in my life. My short and carefree existence had come to an end and I could see nothing but drudgery looming in front of me forever. I do not recall learning very much there either. My writing was a

105

spidery scrawl; I could see what was wrong with it but nothing I did made it better. The high point of my nursery school education was a production of *Hiawatha*. We were asked to bring white chicken feathers that could be painted and made into Red Indian headdresses. I was to be an Indian – not a chief.

Another memory was of Christmas Eve when Mum and Dad had gone to midnight mass. The English nanny had long gone by then so we were left in the charge of the African servants who were having their own celebration with the help of a bottle or two of *waragi* (nubian gin). We were got out of bed and invited to join the festivities. All the oil lamps were lit and our hidden Christmas presents were discovered and unwrapped. We were thrilled to find they included a fairy cycle, the smallest size two-wheeled bicycle of the time. There must have been a scene when our parents returned. I would have been six at the time because I remember being six when I learnt to ride a two-wheeler.

Another much-loved present – Christmas or birthday, I forget which – was a junior carpentry set, some latent talent having been detected in me. I used to delight in remodelling wooden packing crates as crude furniture. Many a time I trod on a nail with my bare feet. (We were not allowed to wear shoes because Dad claimed that whenever we took them off we lost them.) Thus I learned to be careful. I also sawed through the main plank of the seesaw, which was not a popular thing to do.

Some time in the mid-1930s the government decided that Kampala needed an aerodrome, so it bulldozed a piece off the shoulder of Kalolo Hill about three miles away across the valley. When it was finished a few small aeroplanes could be seen from our house taking off and landing. I decided that Mulago should also have an airstrip, so I set about making one. The lawn would have to do, but what I needed was a windsock, so I cut the sleeve off an old shirt and tied it to a pole planted in a flowerbed. After that, I would rush out whenever I heard a plane, but none of them ever landed on Mulago. They must have thought it was too hilly. The real airstrip in fact turned out to be a white elephant and was hardly ever used – at least by aircraft. It did have its uses, however, for most of us learnt to drive on it in our teenage years.

When I was six Dad was promoted to senior medical officer and posted to the Western Province, so we left Mulago for Fort Portal – 200 miles of dirt road away from Kampala. The government laid on a lorry for our furniture, on top of which the servants rode, but how Mum and the girls travelled is a mystery. Michael and I went with Dad and the cat plus lots of luggage. We had a newer car by then – a dark blue Ford V8, which was an improvement on the old canvas-roofed tourer we used to have. The cat travelled in a wicker basket and mewed the whole journey. We stopped for petrol at Mubende, which was a small collection of Indian *duka*s at the halfway point and a very kind *duka wallah* cooked a meal for us.

Being about 6000 feet above sea level, Fort Portal was cooler than Kampala, in fact cold enough to have a log fire at night. Despite the cold, the locals wore no more than skin loincloths and carried spears, though for what purpose I never found out. One advantage of the temperate climate was the profusion of strawberries; a large basket sold at the back door would cost two shillings. We ate them every day – both fresh and as jam –and never got tired of them.

If Fort Portal had been in India it would have been called a hill station. It was certainly hilly and, on rare occasions, the snow-capped Ruwenzori mountains were revealed lit up by the setting sun. They were a magnificent sight and, at 20 square miles, were the most extensive snowfield in Africa.

For me the best thing about Fort Portal was the absence of school (though Mum did her best to provide rudimentary lessons), so I could resume my idyllic childhood and continue the carefree existence Mrs Holmes's academy had so cruelly interrupted. (Why should I learn to read when Margaret could always read to me?) Until Michael was sent to boarding school in Kenya, he and I wandered through the surrounding countryside wherever we wanted to go. It was much wilder than Kampala. An occasional lion or leopard was seen in the neighbourhood but they never bothered us, though they killed the cat. We had long shaken off the control of the *ayah* and Mum and Dad placed no restrictions on us, probably because they could not be enforced.

The provincial commissioner, Mr Dauncey Tongue, and his wife lived next door to us in a very much bigger bungalow than ours and with a thatched guest cottage and rondavel (round thatched hut) in their enormous garden. Her hobby was to grow vegetables and her *bêtes noires* were the mouse birds that ate them. Every evening Michael, her Sealyham dog Bonny and I would accompany her as she stalked around the vegetable garden with a four-ten shotgun with which to shoot them. Any bird that hit the ground alive had not reckoned on Bonny being ready and waiting with a quick bite and shake! It was not long before Michael and I were given turns with the four-ten and so it was that my shooting career started at the age of seven. And she did not just go in for shooting; she also took us fishing in the stream that flowed through the bottom of the valley. We had no fancy tackle, just a bent pin on a piece of string tied to a stick and baited with a black and white caterpillar off the lantana hedge, but it was fun. The first thing I caught was a crab, which gripped the hook tightly with both nippers.

Mrs Tongue may have been lonely with her family having grown up and left, but for some reason she took a liking to the two of us and before long we were living in their rondavel at the end of their front veranda. I can't think how to account for this. It must have been out of the kindness of her heart that she helped our family cope with the polio epidemic. No two little boys were better looked after.

Then there was the episode of the pigeons. When Mrs Tongue decided to go in for pigeon keeping the White Fathers' were commissioned to make a dovecote and Dad was instructed to get some pigeons on one of his many safaris. The dovecote arrived first and it was fixed to two stout poles in the lawn in front of the rondavel. We painted it green and white and it looked very smart. Then Dad arrived with the pigeons. We were out at the time, so not knowing any better he placed them in the dovecote and left them, and before long they took wing. Every hawk in Fort Portal thought Christmas had come. The Tongues fought a rearguard battle with their shotguns but there were just too many hawks. I remember a black sparrow hawk – a particularly rare and handsome species I would come to recognize in later life – being one of the casualties. Dad should not have let the pigeons go until they knew where their home was; their wing feathers should have been cut and they should have been confined until their wings had grown again. In due course, another batch of pigeons was obtained, their wings were clipped and they were introduced to the dovecote. However, we had not considered Bonny who was ready and waiting for any pigeon that fell to the ground. So pigeon keeping was abandoned.

In due course, the Tongues left the station and an era came to an end. Our family moved into their bungalow and Michael and I carried on living in the rondavel as before. To Mum's horror, a far-sighted neighbour gave us an air rifle for Christmas, and so our shooting did not come to an end.

Dad's job took him away on safari, as his tours of inspection were called, for about ten days a month. If it meant staying away overnight in government rest houses he would go on his own, but occasionally, if he were going on a day trip, he would take us with him. Two of these trips stand out in my memory. The first was to Bwamba, behind the

Ruwenzori range and practically in the Congo – real rain-forest country with rushing mountain streams. There was not much to Bwamba as I remember it, but it was a change. In its government dispensary we played with the laboratory guinea pigs when we were not swimming in the beautiful clear stream.

The other trip was to the Kazinga Channel, which joins Lake George to Lake Edward and is in the Queen Elizabeth National Park. Accompanied by Dr Mowat, we joined a party of officers on a launch trip down the channel for a tsetse fly survey, and were thrilled by how many animals we saw from the launch. There were hundreds of hippos in the water and elephants, waterbuck, kob and a profusion of birds on the shore. Dad tried a long shot at an Egyptian goose with no result. On the way home Dr Mowat sat in the passenger seat with Dad's shotgun aimed at guinea fowl and francolin through an opening in the windscreen, but he had to be careful not to shoot anything on the right-hand side of the road because that was in the game reserve. It was not long before we had a couple of brace of fat birds in the car.

Like all good things, our life at Fort Portal came to an end with Dad's home leave. I could not understand why they called it 'home' leave. To me, Uganda was home. We children were kept in ignorance of a wicked plot to dump us in England for the rest of our school days, probably never seeing Africa again. This old colonial custom was the norm in those days, the tropics being considered unhealthy for European children. Fortunately for us, Hitler had other ideas and we did get back after all, but that, as they say, is another story. Hitler's war had a destabilizing effect and undoubtedly accelerated the advance to independence, which I felt was a pity. I am sure most people were happier in those sleepy colonial days than they were under tyrants like Idi Amin and his ilk.

## Channel Island interlude: 1939–40

Our children had come through their illness with relatively few long-term disabilities, but we felt they would benefit from a spell of rehabilitation away from the tropics. So we decided that they and I should stay on in Guernsey after our leave and that Arthur should return alone to Uganda for a short tour. Not even the gathering war clouds made us change our mind, for as in 1914 the general feeling was that, even if the worst were to happen, it would all be over if not by Christmas at least soon after that.

It is easy to be wise after the event, but this was an unfortunate decision; indeed, divine providence must have been urging us to think again. Although we had been able to rent a house for the summer months, our efforts to find one to move into after that period were entirely unsuccessful; nothing even remotely suitable was available either to buy or rent. So, when Arthur was recalled to Uganda a few weeks after the outbreak of war, my parents nobly insisted that the children and I should move in with them.

A safe but dreary winter ensued; then, as one European country after another crumbled before the Nazi advance, the Channel Islands began to look less and less like the haven of peace and safety so many of their inhabitants believed them to be. And when France capitulated it seemed as if a great bulwark had collapsed at our feet, leaving us teetering on the edge of an abyss.

There was panic and confusion everywhere. Although at the time we blamed the authorities for their lack of coherent leadership, I suppose they were as much in the dark as the rest of us on what plans – if any – were being formulated on the mainland (as England was always referred to) for the hundreds of people who wanted to leave the island. Eventually a couple of mail boats came to the rescue, but most people made their getaway – as we did – in cattle (or tomato) boats about three days before the Germans arrived.

111

It was a traumatic experience and during the next couple of months, which we spent in Devonshire, I had to weigh up the pros and cons of remaining in England, where air raids were on the increase, or facing the hazards of a wartime voyage to East Africa with seven children. Eventually, thank God, I made the right decision and, although our travels were protracted and complicated, we were at least spared an encounter with the enemy.

I applied to the Crown Agents for passages on a mail boat rather than in a convoy; rightly or wrongly I regarded the latter as too much of a sitting duck. Our port of embarkation remained a dark secret until the eleventh hour. It was too much to hope that we would be sailing from the south coast, so I was not unduly surprised to find that we had to make our way to Glasgow. The start of our journey was slightly inauspicious because our nearest station, Newton Abbot, had been bombed the previous night and we had to drive first to Exeter. My parents, still very shaken by their abrupt departure from Guernsey, insisted on accompanying us all the way. I am sure when we took leave of each other at a railway hotel that they had grave doubts that they would ever see me again.

The voyage, which might so easily have been fraught with anxiety and danger, proved surprisingly enjoyable. Within a few hours of embarkation we were summoned for boat drill, which was naturally very different from the usual light-hearted performance. As I struggled on deck with the children and our eight cumbersome cork life jackets, I wondered how I would cope should a genuine emergency arise. My anxieties were relieved by three unknown but stalwart men immediately coming forward to say they would regard us as their personal responsibility should the worst happen.

Our ship's zigzag progress across the waves – designed of course to fox the submarines – produced quite the most sick-making conditions of my not inconsiderable experience.

For 24 hours, five of the children and I were beyond caring what happened to us, while Peter, aged nine, took charge of the youngest Jossie (later Jo), who was a rapid mover in her own peculiar crab-like fashion and had a special liking for companionways! Then I dragged my fellow sufferers and myself out of our bunks and we staggered up on deck, where we gradually regained our equilibrium.

The rest of the voyage was surprisingly normal, though rather protracted because we took three weeks to reach the Cape. Inevitably, there was a children's fancy-dress party and, while the older children helped me concoct crêpe paper costumes in which they all eventually appeared as the seven dwarfs, I was reminded of comparable activities in very similar circumstances in 1914.

We had hoped that our ship, the *Arundel Castle*, would take us all the way to Mombasa, but all available shipping was badly needed to convey South African troops to East Africa in anticipation of an Italian attack from the north. So at Cape Town we were transferred to the *Stirling Castle* and taken as far as Durban, where we were left high and dry. In some respects it seemed as if we were swimming against the tide, for a number of families had already been sent to South Africa from East Africa in expectation of an Italian invasion. But Arthur and I had had enough separations and preferred to present a united front to whatever might transpire.

Meanwhile, our chances of continuing the journey were extremely uncertain; we were told that we might wait weeks or even months, probably the latter. This was a daunting prospect, but I must record the wonderful kindness of both officials and private individuals during our enforced sojourn. Refugees, as we were regarded, and rightly I suppose, were a novelty, and I expect our numbers provided added interest, for we were the recipients of much practical assistance (including piles of children's books), which I shall always remember with gratitude.

I had joined forces with a fellow passenger who, with her

small son, was also trying to rejoin her husband in Uganda. We found accommodation together in a hotel in the city while we took stock of the situation, which, in view of the prevailing uncertainties, was no easy task. But within a few days we were very fully employed because my friend's little boy and all my children (in detachments) developed measles. With the appearance of the first spots, we realized that we would have to find more suitable quarters and were lucky to be able to take over the annexe of a seaside hotel near Durban, which was available as it was the 'off' season.

The next few weeks were strenuous and worrying. Some of the children were quite seriously ill and, to make matters worse, the measles was succeeded by bacillary dysentery and an outbreak of head lice. However, as their convalescence progressed I grew increasingly concerned about Michael and Peter who had been running wild for far longer than was good for them; they were badly in need of discipline and schooling. With still no sign of a passage materializing and no knowing how long we would have to stay in South Africa, Arthur and I, having discussed the matter as best we could on paper, decided to send the two boys to St George's College, a Jesuit school in Salisbury in Southern Rhodesia.

This seemed the best thing to do in the circumstances, but as I fitted the boys out for their new school and sadly saw them off on the train to Southern Rhodesia I hoped sincerely that we were acting in their best interests. I suppose it was inevitable that within a few days of their departure we were told that a Dutch ship would shortly be leaving for Mombasa and that, since it was too small for use as a troop carrier, we would be able to travel on it. So, just two months after our arrival in Durban, we were once more on our way.

We had a great sendoff from the many people who had befriended us so kindly. One charming couple who had visited us on several occasions repeated their plea to be allowed to adopt Jossie. However, she clung firmly to the devil she knew while I explained that even with seven children I really had none to spare. Again we had a safe and relatively easy journey but hardly a relaxing one because most of the deck space was without railings and Gillie and Jossie seemed determined to meet a watery grave.

When on arrival in Mombasa we found that we had just missed the twice-weekly train to Uganda and would have to wait there over the weekend, this further delay seemed to be the last straw. It was all the more trying as hoteliers, who were enjoying a boom with so many members of the forces to be accommodated, had no interest at all in a couple of women and a pack of children. Finally, we were told we could fit ourselves into two rooms as best we might, though Gillie – a seasoned traveller at the age of three – nearly wrecked our chances by enquiring in ringing tones, 'Does they have menus in this hotel?' They did not.

We were thankful indeed to board the train for the last leg of what had been a considerable Odyssey, starting five months before with our flight from Guernsey. We were even more thankful to be reunited with Arthur in Kampala and to settle down once more to a normal existence.

## War years in Uganda: 1940-45

By the time we reached Uganda in November 1940, our eldest daughter Margaret was over the tropical school age limit, but naturally such strictures went by the board in the general emergency. The Uganda government had, willy-nilly, bowed to the inevitable and provided a junior school in Kampala where, fortunately, we would be living, for Arthur was now provincial medical officer of Buganda.

In other ways too progress had come to Kampala, for all modern conveniences were now available. Along with these and the fact that the introduction of public health measures had greatly reduced the incidence of malaria, the country's health and living conditions had improved beyond recognition.[3] We even enjoyed the luxury of a large electric fridge, which Arthur had had the foresight to snap up; it must have been the last one in the shops for many a day. He also acquired a very basic Ford V8 box-body vehicle, which, while far from being a status symbol adequately met our large family's needs over the coming years. Two low wooden benches provided the only seats and canvas blinds, which were rolled down in wet weather, protected the long back windows. Access was mainly through the windows!

During the following year we led a rather nomadic life because, after several months in a privately owned house the government had rented to meet a temporary shortage of accommodation, we were moved to a relatively modern, spacious bungalow we hoped would be our permanent abode. However, this was not to be. A newly-arrived puisne judge and his wife, a rather elderly childless couple, had to be housed in accordance with his *katibwa*, so we had to move to an ancient bungalow just like the one we had lived in at Fort Portal. This was destined to be our home for the next 15 years, though alterations and an L-shaped extension eventually improved it a great deal; at least it had the virtue of being conveniently placed for the European and Asian hospitals, where Arthur often worked, and for the school.

Owing to the exigencies of war, most government departments were short staffed. Ironically though, the tempo of development was greatly accelerated, so personnel were being stretched to the full and Arthur was very busy. In addition to his official administrative work in the province, he was in high demand as the only eye specialist in the country with clinics and operating sessions at

---

3. Yet, despite all this, I remember succumbing to malaria soon after our return and very unpleasant it was too (editor).

Mulago, and European and Asian patients fitted in as best he could.

It seemed strange to be living in Uganda in wartime so far from the perils and privations our relatives and friends in England were experiencing. Initially, of course, there had been the threat of an Italian invasion from the north and, had it happened, there would have been little to stop it, though I am sure our local version of Dad's Army would have done its best to defend us. Our air-raid warning system consisted of metal bars hanging on trees to be beaten at the appropriate moment, but as we had no shelters I cannot imagine what use they would have been. As the threat of attack receded, it felt as if we were living in a vacuum almost guiltily immune from hardships. As most of our food came from Kenya, there was little rationing, although imported goods were naturally very few and far between.

Paradoxically, during the years when the rest of the world was engulfed in war, the atmosphere in Uganda was one of peace and freedom. Even a rabid anti-colonialist could not have described the protectorate's administration as oppressive; in a framework of law and order everyone prospered and the nearest thing to hardship anyone had to suffer was the extraction of an annual poll tax of 30 shillings (£1.50). We still seemed blessedly free of political or intertribal tensions; such crimes as were committed were more likely caused by an over indulgence of local brew than by malice or forethought. European families enjoyed complete freedom to come and go with never the thought of a hand being raised against them; and, as burglaries were unheard of, few people locked their doors.

Mail between the United Kingdom and East Africa (and elsewhere no doubt) was irregular and spasmodic; some letters that turned up several months after they had been posted looked as if they had had exciting adventures. The introduction of the airgraph service in April 1941 greatly

117

improved the situation and, although it offered no privacy in one's correspondence, we could at least exchange news with reasonable regularity and speed. An airgraph took the form of a single quarto-sized sheet of paper on which a letter was written, or preferably typed, on one side only; it was then taken, unfolded, to the post office to be photographed, reduced to postage stamp size and dispatched by air. At the other end it was 'blown up' to about a quarter of its original size before being delivered in a special envelope.

While women like us did what we could to help with Red Cross sewing parties and other fund-raising activities, the current governor's wife caused much amusement but made no noticeable difference to the war effort when, in rousing tones, she addressed the European female population as 'ladies of Entebbe' and 'women of Kampala' respectively. Women and ladies alike viewed her efforts more sympathetically when Government House was being redecorated and she tried to change the colour scheme of the Public Works Department's universal 'buff'. She met her match in the foreman who rejected her suggestion out of hand and, with no regard for her status as the wife of a baronet and an 'honourable' told her firmly, 'buff we've got and buff you'll have to have, Misses Dundas!'

Some of us did courses in first aid and home nursing and I even acquired a uniform in which to do some VAD work, but pregnancy intervened so the patients were spared that particular horror of war.

It had been four years since our seventh child was born, so there was almost a touch of novelty in the situation and the children were very excited at the prospect of having a baby in the family. They were so well accustomed to the shortages and restrictions of wartime that, on one occasion, I came upon the two youngest little girls engaged in a heated argument over whether they were each going to have a baby or would have to share as usual! I do not think we would have been unduly perturbed to have had a sixth daughter, but undoubtedly the appearance of a third son, Antony, made a nice change and the little girls were all his devoted slaves. Preparing his layette had posed quite a problem in view of the shortage of all materials. But the *duka*s yielded up a cream-coloured Somali shawl, rather like fine Viyella in texture, which proved ideal for nighties, while matinée jackets were concocted rather in the style of 'Joseph's coat' out of assorted remnants of wool donated by kind friends. There was even a special pleasure in using one's ingenuity in this way and to this day I find it very hard to throw out scraps of material and wool.

When I see all the toys and equipment my grandchildren and their contemporaries take for granted, I am thankful to have brought up my family in less sophisticated times. Presents were only received at birthdays and Christmas and they were then, as far as possible, things that were really wanted and looked forward to with eager anticipation. Our children's amusements were mostly of their own devising, and parties with homegrown entertainments like treasure hunts and competitions were keenly enjoyed. An important part of giving parties for younger children was the *ayahs*' tea, for which no elaborate catering was involved but generous supplies of bread, jam, tea, sugar and milk ensured the success of the occasion; one could always gauge the reputation of a hostess by the enthusiasm or otherwise with which news of an invitation was received.

For older children going to the 'flicks' was a great treat, though not one without hazard, for rats frequently joined the audience – actually jumping onto the lap of one young friend and snapping a chocolate bar out of the fingers of another! For a time another cinema made its appearance in 'temporary' premises consisting of a large tent. I cannot imagine how the authorities allowed films to be shown in such a dangerous venue, but they did and I was among the large, spellbound audience that endured its stuffy discomfort for a marathon showing of *Gone With the Wind*.

Amateur theatricals and concerts came into their own at a time when the audiences could not go on leave, so were starved of the genuine article. I look back in amazement on the roles I played with more temerity than skill. I was also a member of a small orchestral group (that cello had not travelled to Africa in vain) that met weekly for our own amusement and put on a series of very popular concerts at the Kampala Club. I expect our efforts were good for morale at a time when life was drab if not dangerous and various war charities benefited to a modest extent. Social life had become less formal. Buffet suppers replaced starchy dinners and, although dinner jackets and evening frocks were worn on those occasions, they no longer featured in the home circle. Even the great divide between senior and junior officials had become slightly blurred at the edges.

Meanwhile, we were managing to get Michael and Peter from Rhodesia by rather roundabout air travel for their long holidays, which came at Christmas time. A farming family some distance from Salisbury quite happily catered for their two shorter holidays, but later this arrangement broke down and in other ways we felt they would be better nearer home. So from 1945 they went as boarders to the Prince of Wales School in Nairobi, which had developed rapidly to meet the current need. All this is anticipating events, but with a large family it is not easy to keep a strictly chronological account. During this period our daughters were moving off one by one to the Loreto Convent – evacuated from Nairobi to Lumbwa in the Kenya Highlands when the FANYs requisitioned its building. Though classrooms and dormitories had to be improvised, the main part of the temporary school had been the hunting lodge of an Austrian aristocrat; nonetheless, the children were well cared for and good academic standards were maintained. They came and went by train, a journey they greatly enjoyed, and we fortunately were spared the upheavals and expense of the lengthy half terms and free weekends that nowadays seem to make up a disproportionate part of so-called boarding school life.

The use of petrol was of course restricted, but occasionally we took a weekend jaunt to Kazi, on the lakeshore about ten miles from Kampala, where the sailing club had its moorings. There were a number of keen yachtsmen there, including Arthur, but the only boat I really enjoyed sailing in was a converted war canoe, owned by 'Staps' (E. G. Staples), the sailing club's founder and leading light. I think that my liking for this rather strange craft was because little was expected of ignorant crew members like me other than that we endeavour to keep the boat trimmed by sitting out on the outriggers while enjoying the breeze.

Another popular outing was to the swimming pool in Entebbe. It was then the only pool in the country and it owed its existence to the initiative of Aubrey Forsyth-Thompson who had been in the Entebbe secretariat some years previously. It was attractively situated on a bluff overlooking the lake, though it was frustrating to look down on that vast and seemingly benign expanse of water and not be able to make use of it. This was because of the ever-present threat of crocodiles and, although some people allowed their children to bathe near the beach where the water was clear, I could never do so with any peace of mind. Later, even the suggestion of a paddle became taboo when the children nearly stepped on a slumbering croc at the foot of a path leading from the pool to the beach. In due course it was discovered that the waters contained yet another menace, namely the snail that plays host to the bilharzia parasite.

The deceptive beauty of Lake Victoria was only one of Uganda's paradoxes. A seemingly perfect climate lacked the stimulus of change and the glorious sunshine could easily prove to be too much of a good thing. Even a balmy night with a full moon could not really be enjoyed out of doors because of the incessant whine of mosquitoes and, in some places, those all-pervading lake flies. I even recall hearing of a romantic moonlit proposal being all but wrecked by the untimely intrusion of stink ants.

Although, as I have said, Uganda's climate was remarkably good in relation to its geographical position, the lack of seasonal change made for monotony and fatigue. So, with home leave out of the question, most people were glad of an occasional holiday in Kenya.

One of our holidays was spent at a place called Diani, on the coast not far from Mombasa, where a reef protected miles of glorious sands and provided a fascinating field of marine exploration at low tide. Kenya's coastal areas have been developed as 'resorts' in recent years with luxury hotels and facilities for water sports, but in our day we stayed in a simple guesthouse and our enjoyment of sea and sands was quite unsophisticated.

We spent another holiday at Hudson-Cain's very pleasant country club cum hotel at Limuru in the Kenya Highlands. Rondavel-type accommodation was grouped around a central building in large and attractive gardens containing tennis courts and a nine-hole golf course. At an altitude of 7300 feet, the air was wonderfully cool and invigorating and in the evenings we revelled in the novelty of huge log fires. Limuru lies in the heart of Kikuyuland, but any thought of the Mau Mau insurrections that were to erupt within a few years were very far from our minds.

Nabugabo, a supposedly crocodile-free lake near Masaka, was a more accessible holiday spot and a few cottages were available for letting. But, though the children enjoyed swimming and paddling about in canoes, the thickly wooded setting was oppressive and there was no climate change from which to benefit. At this point I must anticipate events to relate how, in the late 1940s, Nabugabo suddenly lost its crocodile immunity. It was thought that the invasion – for it was no less – followed a season of unusually heavy rain when the narrow strip of land dividing the little lake from

Lake Victoria became submerged. I still sometimes have nightmares imagining those terrifying creatures lurking in the wings while our children are so happily disporting themselves in the water.

Not surprisingly, Nabugabo ceased to be a holiday spot and when, some years later, I revisited it briefly with some of our family the forest had encroached on the cottages, which were in a state of disintegration. There was a general air of depression from which we were glad to escape.[4]

It was not only in East Africa that the thrilling news of the Normandy landings brought an over-optimistic feeling that the end of the war was imminent. Those last months seemed interminable until May 1945 brought the rejoicings of VE Day. The following month we had a more personal reason to rejoice with the birth of our ninth child and fourth son, David.

In the unspeakable relief of VJ Day I doubt if many people were aware of the full horror of the atom bomb, or of its terrible significance to all future life, which must be lived in the knowledge that the means of total extermination is, only too literally, at hand.

## Postwar Uganda: 1945–56

In East Africa we shared the general sense of relief at the ending of the war, but the actual impact of peace was inevitably far less dramatic for us than it was for those who, for six long years, had endured the threat and actuality of bombings and had lived through the general dreariness and frustrations of shortages, restrictions and blackouts. Nonetheless, it was a relief to know that we were again in close touch with the outer world. It was

---

4. My sister Pauline has since been told that the cottages were repaired and are still very much in use, and that a Baganda music teacher friend of hers goes there frequently with his family (editor).

wonderful too to be able to correspond freely once more with relatives and friends, to be able to think in terms of home leave before very long and even to see a few favourites reappear on the grocer's shelves.

The postwar years were a time of change for everyone and no less so for us in East Africa. On the personal side the first change came with my husband's appointment – at last – as ophthalmic specialist at a salary of £1000, and other specialists received similar recognition. There had been great advances in medicine and surgery during the war years, largely due to the discovery and development of penicillin and antibiotics and improved techniques in anaesthesia. With a very welcome influx of experienced surgeons and physicians to the medical department and medical school, the scope and standards of treatment improved beyond recognition locally as elsewhere.

Other government departments also benefited from an infusion of new blood, though the fact that newcomers were appointed on contracts inevitably meant that some of them regarded a tour in Uganda with its sunshine and servants as a delightful spree after wartime stringencies and had no real interest in the country or its peoples.

With enlarged government departments, more personnel at the university and an expansion of commercial firms, the European population seemed to quadruple overnight. There were strange faces everywhere and, with improved shopping facilities (including a few boutiques), modern cinemas and even a couple of nightclubs, Kampala suddenly lost its village atmosphere.

Coinciding with Kampala's metamorphosis from village to town, a postwar influx of electrical appliances made life at the domestic level much more streamlined. We had come to take electricity, fridges and even modern sanitation very much for granted, but the sudden appearance in our lives of cookers, immersion heaters and washing machines had the impact almost of an industrial revolution.

124

Inevitably, people needed fewer servants in their homes, though with so many more potential employers there were still plenty of domestic jobs for those who wanted them. The first casualty in large households like ours was the *toto jikoni*. With an electric cooker and water heater, there was no longer a need for a hewer of wood and carrier of bath water, though quite a few *mpishi*s were a bit shaken to find that henceforth they would have to do all the cooking.

Our *dhobi* was always a busy man and, even when I acquired Kampala's first-ever washing machine (a basic Hoover with a hand wringer), we had no intention of dispensing with his services. He had been delighted to exchange his clumsy, charcoal-filled iron for an electric one, but a washing machine was another matter altogether, and I was told indignantly that if he were expected to be a mechanic he would have to be paid accordingly! The trouble was that the poor chap saw an end to his soap 'perks'. But in time he came to appreciate our new toy and even regarded it as a status symbol.

In any case servants' wages were rising and, by the time we left Uganda in 1956, our monthly total was 600/– (£30) divided among four, where once we had shared out 160/– (£8) among twice that number. It is only fair to say that over a span of ten years government salaries had also leapt ahead, with my husband's reaching £2600 by 1956. Over the same period we had had to accustom ourselves to the rigours of income tax, which came into being early in 1946.

At that time a joke went around that the government would have to pay the Boases because of all the child allowances, but in practice it was very different, for we could only claim for a maximum of four children – a provision that was really intended to cover Asians who, because of polygamy, probably doubled our total.

Although short-term appointments were a straw in the wind, there was still no talk locally of independence for the

East African territories. And, incredible though it now seems, there could have been no serious thought at the Colonial Office of such a thing happening in the near future, for ex-servicemen were being positively encouraged to buy farms in the Kenya Highlands. However, change was increasingly apparent among the Africans and, though much of it came from the increase in educational opportunities, the process was accelerated by the return of Africans who had had their horizons widened by overseas service with the British forces. Russia had been our glorious ally so recently that I doubt if many people thought in terms of communist propaganda at that time, but I expect it was already at work and that our local malcontents were ideally receptive material.

Our former happy sense of security was undermined when burglaries became a nightly occurrence. Bicycles, radios and even cars were being carried off almost literally from under their owners' noses and it was no longer considered advisable for women to be left on their own, as I had so often been in prewar Fort Portal. Since the wire netting that enclosed our bungalows was ineffective in keeping out intruders, it was reinforced with crisscrossed expanded metal, which gave our homes a strangely old-world appearance.

During one period of unrest, the *Uganda Herald*'s press was sabotaged, presumably because an editorial leader had given offence. Michael Moses, who owned the paper, was so furious about this action that it put paid to my efforts to get him to make an endowment to Makerere College in his will. He had often told me that he saw no reason why his relatives in Baghdad, whom he frequently referred to as a plague of locusts, should reap all the benefits of his labours, so I had hoped there might be a tangible memorial to his long association with Uganda. But after this episode he flatly refused to entertain the idea.

Like the proverbial ill wind, the war brought some good to us and to other parents in East Africa. It spared us those

10. Alice Boase with her five daughters (two sons in background),
Kampala, Uganda, 1949.

traumatic partings that had previously been the great trial of
colonial life. Providentially, the war years coincided with
huge improvements in health and general amenities, at least
in the main centres, but Uganda's climate was as enervating
as ever, so it was just as well that the children had to go to
Kenya for their secondary education, where in general it was
a good deal cooler. To the best of my knowledge those
young people were none the worse off, either scholastically
or in health, for their tropical upbringing. Although, like the
rest of us, they missed out on cultural opportunities, these
were then less generally available even in Western countries
than they are now.

There were no training facilities for Europeans in East
Africa. Although Makerere University was open to all races,
its facilities would not at that time have been congenial to
Europeans. And there were few openings in postwar Britain,
where priority was rightly given to ex-servicemen. So, in the
late 1940s, with the older members of our family growing
up, we had personal problems. Our two eldest sons would

127

11. Alice and Arthur Boase with eight of their ten children, Kampala, Uganda, 1949.

have liked nothing better than to have emulated their friend and hero Captain Charles Pitman, the game warden who generously shared his deep love and knowledge of wild life with them and other young enthusiasts. However, not everyone can turn a hobby into a career, let alone with such distinction, so Michael and Peter had to turn their thoughts to more practical propositions.

Michael surprised us by opting out of the professional tradition, so strong on both sides of the family, and embarking on a career in the East African business world. Our second son, Peter, eventually trained as an engineer through an apprenticeship with a firm in Derby; later on our two eldest daughters, Margaret and Gemma, followed in my footsteps to the finishing school in Switzerland. Having undergone a brief period of resuscitation after the war, it provided our two daughters with a beneficial break between an East African upbringing and training in London as a secretary and nurse respectively.

The pattern of overseas leave was gradually resumed and

air travel became the norm, but we seemed to have got past wanting to go home. Though I am sure we were badly in need of a break from the tropics after so many years, it was impractical to think of taking our large family to England in the immediate postwar period. I was particularly anxious to see my parents who were getting on in years, but they solved that problem by deciding to visit us in Uganda in 1947. They came in August, ostensibly for three months, but on hearing that our tenth child was due in November they agreed to stay on for the event. So it was that our youngest child and their youngest grandchild became my father's namesake, Charles. Against all the odds we had evened the score with five sons and five daughters.

The following year, 1948, Arthur was prevailed on to take a few months much-needed leave on his own, and two years later I followed suit, but more of that later.

Uganda's big social event in 1948 was undoubtedly the Kabaka's wedding. Mutesa had been educated at Budu, the local 'Eton' run by the Church Missionary Society, and was then sent to England where he spent some years at Magdalene College, Cambridge.

He returned to Uganda in October 1948 by sea, under the wing of the resident of Buganda, Lachie Boyd, a kindly but solemn man whose young protégé may well have felt that he took his responsibilities too seriously. I imagine the choice of a sea passage rather than air was expressly intended to give Lachie an opportunity to coach the young man on his future behaviour and duties, but they seem to have enjoyed an amicable relationship. Lachie always maintained that on several occasions Mutesa had spoken enthusiastically about his forthcoming marriage to Damali, the daughter of one of Buganda's leading families who had been handpicked and educated to play her part as *Nabagerika*. The marriage was celebrated the following month at Namirembi Cathedral amid much pomp and circumstance. But I fear little happiness lay in store for the couple as his interest quickly strayed to Damali's sister, Sara, with whom he had a longstanding liaison and several children. Damali had a daughter, Dorothy, and some years later a son, Henry.

## Uganda in the 1950s: 1950–54

The 1950s in Uganda were destined to be eventful both personally and for the country as a whole. Though again I find it hard to keep events in chronological order, at least I have no difficulty recalling that the spring of 1950 saw me setting off on my own for my first overseas leave in nearly ten years.

I suppose I should be ashamed to say with what pleasure I threw off my domestic cares – for the first time ever – and embarked on the novel experience of having absolutely no one but myself to consider for three whole months. Air was by then the usual form of travel and, as my holiday coincided with the Holy Year, my first long flight was to Rome, where I followed the usual pilgrims' round before going on to Switzerland to visit Margaret and my old school. Much of my holiday was spent with my parents in Guernsey, but I also visited relatives and friends in different parts of the United Kingdom and greatly enjoyed a week's orgy of shopping and going to the theatre in London. My absence, incidentally, was made possible by the quite unusual reliability of Gemma, by then the eldest daughter at home, who was well able to cope with the household.

Perhaps because of the sudden widening of my horizons, when I returned to Uganda life seemed very dull indeed. But I think other colonial wives would agree with me that, as our families grew up, and even our three musketeers were doing just that, we simply did not have enough to do. The colonial service has always been a man's world, all the more so for those like my husband who had it both ways, being really interested in his work and an enthusiastic golfer. I had never been particularly good at games and the fact that my participation in them over the years had, of necessity, been intermittent, had not helped. I was fortunate in that music and occasional dramatics provided a little interest outside the home and I have always been a voracious reader, but mind-stretching pursuits were otherwise few and far between. However, as I must now describe, relief was at hand from a totally unexpected quarter.

Over the years my husband served on numerous committees and had been president or chairman of several groups, including professional organizations, the Civil Servants' Association and social clubs. He was also a member of the Kampala Township Authority and when it was upgraded to a municipality he became its first chairman of public health. I had always taken these activities of his for granted, but had assumed that my own role was purely domestic. So it was with considerable diffidence that I agreed to join a seemingly innocuous committee. I then discovered that committees are as catching as measles and, before I knew where I was, I was going the rounds of half a dozen and discovering to my surprise that I not only enjoyed the process but that life was becoming a great deal more interesting. A further surprise was in store when I was asked to join the municipality and this I found very interesting indeed, especially my membership of the planning committee, for at that time of rapid development we seemed to be gaining a glimpse of tomorrow's world. Another aspect of my new work, which I appreciated, was that at last I had an opportunity to get to know members of other racial groups. This was especially true of my connection with the Uganda Council of Women and it was heart warming to find how much we had in common, particularly with regard to the hopes and fears of family life.

It was in 1952, with the arrival of Sir Andrew Cohen as governor, that tomorrow's world seemed to burst upon us. His predecessors had all been career colonial officials who had worked their way up, boy and man, through the ranks of the administration, gaining in the process a considerable understanding of the intricacies of the local people's way of life and thought and the complexities of intertribal relationships. Sir Andrew was a very different proposition. His was a political appointment by the Labour government, which sent him out with a clear mandate to make all possible speed towards independence – a mandate, I might add, that was very much in tune with his own inclinations. Up to this time a handful of elder statesman-type Africans had served on the Legislative Council and municipality, but now there was to be a great acceleration in their participation in public affairs.

The year 1952 also saw the return of my brother Bowes and Eva to Uganda. They had happy memories of the time they had spent there during the 1920s and 1930s and, in taking up his appointment as chief justice, my brother was following in the footsteps of our father who had held this office during much of that earlier period. A very important aspect of this new posting was that his work in this peaceful and prosperous country seemed likely to comply with his medical advisers' insistence that, after his hectic spells in Palestine and Hong Kong, a less stressful atmosphere and work schedule was desirable.

Uganda was certainly peaceful and prosperous. In the light of the appalling troubles that have beset the country and its unfortunate people since the early 1970s, it is ironic that, in trying to describe life as it was during the long years of our family's association with the protectorate, I often wished there had been an outstanding moment, or even an occasional crisis, to enliven the scene. As it was, one smiling sunny day succeeded another in seemingly endless succession and my brother agrees with me that, though our living conditions were pleasant, they lacked any variety and excitement from which to weave a dramatic narrative.

There was in fact to be just one event that hit the headlines. This was the deportation of the Kabaka, and the subsequent repercussions, which culminated in what came to be known as the 'Kabaka case', of which more anon.

While Uganda was feeling the effects of Sir Andrew's new broom, dreadful events were taking place in neighbouring Kenya, where the eruption of the Mau Mau rebellion was bringing death and mutilation to black and white alike, and unspeakable degradation to its mainly Kikuyu perpetrators. In Uganda we were mercifully free from the violence of this manifestation, but it had its sympathizers and there were increasing signs of nationalist stirrings. Like other parents, our main concern was for the safety of our children at school in Kenya; at one time it looked as if they would have to be brought back to be given makeshift schooling in Kampala and Jinja, the two largest centres. This would have involved finding accommodation for those whose homes were upcountry, which was not easy because few of us were well endowed with spare bedrooms. Eventually, it was decided that, as the schools were very well protected by British troops and the main danger lay in the possibility of sabotage on the railways, the pupils would henceforth travel back and forth by air.

By 1953 the Africanization programme was proceeding apace. A decision to enlarge the Legislative Council from 32 to 57 members in 1954 brought more Africans into central government. At the same time, the governor was busy with preliminary plans for the country's independence in the foreseeable future, in which a unitary state with a central legislature elected on a constituency basis along party-political lines was envisaged. It was here that Sir Andrew found himself up against the Kabaka (Mutesa II) whose opposition arose because he was concerned about the likely fate of the Kingdom of Buganda and of its hereditary ruler when Uganda became independent. In the protracted negotiations that followed the Kabaka stuck to his guns and even pressed for secession and separate independence for his little king-

12. Sir John Griffin in his robes *circa* 1962.

dom, which was hardly a realistic demand but no doubt a measure of his desperation. Who now, in the light of future developments, can say that his fears were unfounded?

However, the governor and Uganda government (with

the support of Her Majesty's government in London acting through the Colonial Office) were equally determined that independence must come to Uganda as a united state. The Kabaka was abruptly notified that his recognition as king of Buganda had been withdrawn and he was summarily exiled to the UK by RAF aircraft. The shock to his Baganda people can be imagined.[5]

Indeed, the suddenness and severity of this action shook us all. The Kabaka's exile lasted for over a year and ended only because he and his advisers won their case in the Uganda high court. The chief justice (at that time my brother, Sir John Griffin) heard the 'Kabaka case', as it was popularly known. Following a long hearing at which leading Queen's Counsel (Messrs Diplock and Dingle Foot) from England appeared for the Kabaka, the chief justice held that the governor, the Uganda government and HMG had wrongly exiled the Kabaka by misapplying Article 6 of the 1900 Uganda Agreement, which required that the Kabaka, his chiefs and people should fail together in loyal cooperation with the government, whereas as the court so found only the Kabaka had failed to cooperate.

The 'Kabaka case' was followed by an amendment to the Uganda Agreement of 1900 and by the return of the Kabaka from exile to his kingdom of Buganda, to await Uganda's independence in October 1962 as a unified state of which he was designated president. In view of his earlier misgivings, he can have had little sense of security in this office and his premonitions were tragically fulfilled when he had to flee the country and seek sanctuary in England. The few remaining years of his life were spent in very straitened

---

5. I vividly recall seeing grieving Baganda men, including our *dhobi* Isaaki, growing beards in protest at the deportation. It was reported that on the Kabaka's return he was presented with cushions stuffed with their shaved-off hair (editor).

circumstances, though these were mitigated to some extent by the personal generosity of a few British friends – among them a former governor of Uganda. He died in the East End of London in November 1969, aged only 44, in what some people thought were suspicious circumstances.

Again I have anticipated events, for early in 1954 the newly-constituted Legislative Council came into being, but with the *Lukiko* refusing to cooperate over the appointment of Buganda members, it went less smoothly than His Excellency had visualized. Apart from nine ex-officio members, the Legislative Council was still a nominated assembly, although the district councils elected 11 of the 20 African members, albeit subject to the governor's approval. Several Africans became ministers virtually overnight, but former directors of the various departments, known henceforth as permanent secretaries, supported them in the Legislative Council and elsewhere.

Another innovation was the cross-bench, consisting, and I quote from Dr Ingham's book *The Making of Modern Uganda*, 'of about ten leading and respected members of the public', and here, to my amazement, I found myself installed. I actually had the honour of being the first woman to take the oath in the Legislative Council, but I must hasten to add that my seniority was purely alphabetical, as another and far more worthy lady parliamentarian, Barbara Saben, also took the oath that day. I think the governor appointed me for no better reason than that he wanted to establish the principle of having women members and saw in me, through sheer length of residence in Uganda, a sort of elder states-woman of a non-controversial sort.

It had been hoped that the cross-bench would provide a sort of balance between official and unofficial factions. In general, we were free to speak and vote as we pleased, though we were expected to vote with the government should matters of confidence arise. In practice, we seemed to be neither fish nor fowl, and we were thankful when, after a

13. Town Hall, Kampala, Uganda 1950s, where Legislative Council meetings were held until the Parliament/National Assembly was built in 1962.

year, the cross-bench was abolished and we retreated to the backbenches on either side of the house. I was in the government ranks and rather loosely attached to the minister for education, on whose behalf I occasionally asked a question or made a minor intervention. My speeches were few and unremarkable and my only real contribution was towards improving the council chamber's ventilation – and this I achieved when wearing my municipal 'hat'. At that time Legislative Council met in the Kampala town hall, one of a group of buildings that seemed to owe its architectural inspiration to Noah's Ark. By suggesting that a couple of windows, which rather strangely had been designed not to open, should be altered, honourable members became less likely to nod off during lengthy sessions.

The year 1954 brought three notable events to our family. The first of these was the departure of our daughter

Pauline to Pretoria, where she joined the Loreto novitiates. Because of her position in the family as the middle of five daughters she had once been referred to by another as 'the one who hasn't got anyone', and certainly her choice of career has been unique but in every way fulfilling.

The next event was our silver wedding, which our family celebrated in great style, although by that time only three of our children were still in Uganda. Soon after that our eldest daughter, Margaret, married Eric Knowlden, who was working at that time for an engineering firm in Kampala.

The same year brought a royal visit to Uganda, which caused the usual flutter in the dovecotes. This was Queen Elizabeth's second visit to the country, but the first had been unscheduled and in tragic circumstances. As Princess Elizabeth, she and Prince Philip were in Kenya when the news of her father's death reached them and they flew to Entebbe to connect as quickly as possible with a plane sent from England to bring them home. Unfortunately, their arrival coincided with one of Entebbe's spectacular storms and they were grounded for several hours during the night, while thunder and lightning crashed and flashed around them. It is to be hoped that the Queen has happier memories of her second visit, but it came at the end of a long and gruelling tour through Australia and New Zealand and, although the Duke was as ebullient as ever, she looked very tired and thin. Nonetheless, the official round went on and included the inauguration of the Owen Falls Dam at the source of the Nile, which had been the *raison d'être* of the visit. The country was going through a period of unrest at the time and for this reason it was decided to fly the royal party between Entebbe and Jinja. Thus, the Queen never saw the elaborate arches the various racial groups had erected along the road, including one that bore the words 'GOD SAVE THE QUEEN FROM THE GOAN COMMUNITY'!

In the summer of 1955 we had our first postwar family leave, although by then we only had the four youngest to take home with us, for their elders were spreading their wings in different ways and places. Three of the older ones were in England, Peter still with the engineering firm in Derby, Gemma training at St Thomas' Hospital and Gillie completing a year's house-craft schooling at Ascot, so the house we rented in Hampshire tended to fill up at the weekends.

From my point of view this was a kind of baptism of fire, for it was only at this stage, at the age of 45, that I had to cook the family meals. Thankfully, I found I could cope and we all survived, but since those experimental days I cannot say that cooking has ever worried me unduly – though, like many an ex-colonial lady, I have never really achieved a close relationship with a vacuum cleaner and duster.

At this time we were experiencing some anxiety about our future. Arthur had long exceeded the length of service required to qualify for a maximum pension, but with a lot of butter still needed for the family bread there could be no question of actual retirement, even if it had been desired. Many people urged him to go into private practice in Uganda, but I viewed the prospect with dismay because I had always been averse to the idea of growing old in Africa. Our uncertainties were resolved in an unexpected way. While we were in England Arthur was invited to apply for the post of warden of the ophthalmic hospital of the Order of St John in Jerusalem, which would fall vacant in July 1956. When Arthur told me about the offer – typically saying that the decision was up to me – I felt as if our prayers had been answered. I had always longed to visit the Holy Land and to be going there to live seemed too good to be true. Arthur, however, though much more attached to Uganda than I had ever been, was attracted to the idea of working in a hospital that had earned a big reputation over a period of 70 years.

In due course, the appointment was confirmed and we returned to Uganda for nine final months, during which we had gradually to relinquish our connections with local affairs. It was amusing – even mildly flattering – to find that people of all races viewed our departure with surprised dismay; they had apparently come to regard us as the local Rock of Ages.

Strangely, one of my main concerns at that time was the future of our old friend, Michael Moses. By then he was in his early eighties, in indifferent health, extremely deaf and increasingly lonely, for all his friends were leaving Uganda. The prospect of our departure distressed him very much and it seemed to me that it would be better for him to return to his relatives in Iraq. Although in moments of exasperation he had thought of them as a plague of locusts, I felt sure that to them he was the goose that laid the golden egg and, as such, would give him the care and respect to which he was entitled. Tentatively, I put forward the suggestion and found to my relief that his thoughts had been moving along similar lines. Thankfully, the plan worked out successfully and his few remaining years were spent in a suitably patriarchal setting.

In the autumn of that year (1955) the Kabaka returned from exile under the provisions of a new Buganda Agreement. The governor, seemingly under the impression that bygones were bygones, was ready to greet him at Entebbe airport with a happy smile and an outstretched hand, but Mutesa ignored both.

I was present at the signing of the new agreement, which took place with much solemnity. I found it difficult to glean, in the thick of all the legal verbiage, in just what respects it differed from the original document and have a sneaking impression that it amounted to little more than a face-saving exercise for all concerned.

And so we moved into 1956 and into our final months in Uganda, which had been our home for so long. Inevitably, there were mixed feelings, for this had been the birthplace of all but two of our ten children and it had given them all, I think, a singularly happy setting for their childhood – and in most cases towards and into adult life. Nonetheless, with development the country had become much more sophisticated and, though we had been grateful for the many improvements in health and living standards, Africa stripped of its simplicity had lost much of its charm and seemed increasingly to resemble a slice of tropical suburbia.

Anyone who has served overseas will know that farewell parties and gifts are occupational risks. We were very touched by the kindness and generosity of our friends, while secretly congratulating ourselves that, unlike the Anglican bishop and his wife who had retired some years previously, our luggage did not have to include 27 African drums![6]

## Postscript

We left Uganda in June 1956, but our departure did not mean the end of our association with East Africa – nor, indeed, of our family's colonial connection.

In 1958, our daughter Gillian went back to Uganda as a secretary with the Uganda Electricity Board and the following year I flew from Jerusalem to attend her wedding to Keith Brian-Boys, a civil engineer also working for the Uganda Electricity Board. She was 'given away' by our eldest son Michael who, having worked for the African Mercantile Company in various parts of East Africa, had returned to Uganda as the representative of a Kenya firm of coffee brokers and later went into business there on his own. Also at the wedding were my brother and his wife, for although he had retired from the chief justiceship in 1956, he returned to Kampala early in 1958 as the first ever

---

6. Alice and Arthur Boase spent 13 very happy years in Jerusalem. Alice has recorded their experiences in *We Reach the Promised Land*.

Speaker in the Legislative Council, over which the governor had previously presided, and later of the National Assembly. Meanwhile, our second son Peter was working in Tanganyika as an engineer with a Danish sugar concern and he later spent some years in the Sudan in a similar capacity.

My second visit to East Africa, in 1962, was chiefly to see Pauline who had returned to Kenya after seven years as a Loreto novitiate in Pretoria, but I also spent some days in Kampala with Gillian and Keith who were shortly to move to New Zealand. This visit coincided with Uganda's independence when, it is ironic to note, the hand of a certain Idi Amin lowered the Union Jack. I doubt if any country has ever achieved independence in such felicitous circumstances: the transfer had taken place without even a vestige of friction and, if any doubts lingered in the bosom of the Kabaka – now president of the new state – he kept them to himself. Uganda was peaceful and prosperous and the future seemed full of smiling promise.

Shortly after my husband's retirement from Jerusalem in 1969 we revisited our old stamping ground together and found it a disillusioning experience. Our eldest son Michael was still in Kampala but inevitably most of our friends had left and, although there were still a number of Europeans working for the government and for commercial firms, they all had an air of impermanence about them and seemed to steer a wary course.

We were particularly struck by a sense of insecurity, which was expressed in various ways: robbery with violence was prevalent and we were advised against hiring a car to get about the country as we had hoped to do because of the likelihood of encountering bandits on the roads. The Asians were particularly insecure, for even before Idi Amin came to power the government was playing a cat-and-mouse game with them, and they simply did not know from one month to the next if their trading licences would be renewed. It was now very different from the peaceful, happy country we had

14. Alice and Arthur Boase in retirement, Maresfield, Sussex, 1970s.

known and we had no desire to extend our scheduled ten-day visit.

Our eldest son and his wife left Uganda in 1971 and, in

view of the appalling developments of the last decade, we are thankful we no longer have a stake in that unfortunate country.

Our East African link is maintained, however, through our daughter Pauline. For several years she has been head-mistress of Loreto Msongari, the large convent school in Nairobi she and our other daughters attended in the 1940s and 1950s.

At that time the pupils were exclusively European, but now the numbers are divided fairly equally between Africans, Asians and Europeans, and, in this particular league of nations, peace and harmony reign – a happy example the rest of the world might do well to follow.

We no longer speak of 'colonies', but nonetheless a few fragments of empire remain. So it is through our daughter Gillian and her husband Keith Brian-Boys, who was with the Ministry of Works in Hong Kong for several years, that in the 1980s we still maintained a connection with an all but vanished way of life.

# 3

# John Bowes and Eva Griffin

For my brother, John Bowes, the Nyasaland life familiar to him as a small boy ended when he was left in Dublin in the care of his formidable paternal grandmother at the age of seven, so that he could go to school. The top-floor nursery had barred windows and he shared it with me, still only a baby. Our sister, Kathleen, was the only one taken abroad at that stage with our parents. Bowes remembered being miserably cold that first winter, and homesick for Blantyre, to the extent that the sight of the man with the barrel organ and monkey seemed like a link with home. The adults of the household of course found the noise produced by the organ intolerable, so the glimpse of the monkey only lasted until a maid was sent out with sixpence for the man and the request that he should move on.

Granny Griffin died in 1911. Without much counselling, eight-year-old Bowes was treated as 'principal mourner' and seated in solitary state in the first carriage behind the hearse, which six black horses pulled from the southern part of Dublin across the Liffey to the burial in the cemetery north of the river. He had no idea what was to happen to him and me. In due course we were transferred to our maternal grandmother's house, which was where we lived until 1912 when our parents returned to Ireland on leave. Kathleen and I then accompanied them on their return to Africa, leaving only Bowes at school.

In 1914 we moved to Gibraltar, where Bowes and a few other boys travelled to join their parents for the summer holidays in 1915. The outward journey across France with their chaperone cum tutor took them to Marseilles, where they joined a ship to Gibraltar. The war situation deteriorated and civilian travel was stopped, so the boys had an extended stay with their families. An army officer, Charles Seymour Mullan, who had been badly wounded in France, partially filled this gap in his formal education by giving him Greek and Latin lessons. A few years later Charles Mullan joined the Indian Civil Service and married our sister Kathleen.

Eventually, it became possible for Bowes to return to Clongowes, his Jesuit school in Ireland with excellent teaching but a rigorous and Spartan regime. Our mother recalled equipping him with the required three pairs of sheets only to find, on unpacking when he left the school, one well-used pair and two still in their cellophane wrappers. Meanwhile, Kathleen and I stayed with our parents in the West Indies until our father was transferred to Uganda. We then had a brief taste of boarding school while Bowes went to university.

With such a large family it was perhaps as well that we did not have to pack up every few years and set off for some distant corner of the empire. Nonetheless, I greatly envied the variety of places and experiences my brother's different postings brought to him and his family. Sadly, and largely because our leaves failed to coincide and virtually no leaves were possible during and immediately after the war years, we did not meet between 1936 and 1952. This I very much regretted as I had always enjoyed what the politicians would call a special relationship with my unusually kind and tolerant older brother.

To family and friends my brother was always known by his second name, Bowes. So when by a strange coincidence I married Arthur Boase, whose name though spelt differently is pronounced in a similar manner, there were inevitable complications. Our African servants, at any rate, found a simple way around the difficulty by referring to my brother and his wife as *Bwana* and *Memsahib* Bowes, while my husband and I were known as *Bwana* and *Memsahib Doktari.*

I have described my parents' sense of homecoming when they returned to Africa after an absence of seven years, and I am sure Bowes shared that feeling when he took up his first appointment as a cadet in the Uganda administration in 1927. In his case, 17 years had intervened since he left Nyasaland and his memories were inevitably the idealized ones of childhood. But he would have found much that was familiar in Uganda's climatic, social and domestic setting and, with education beyond the primary stage still very much for the elite, even the local people would not have changed very much. Perhaps the main difference between Nyasaland in 1910 (when he left it) and Uganda in 1927 was the improved speed and scope for mobility brought about by the motorcar. In all, I should say, his memories of Uganda at that time coincided fairly closely with my own; but of course he had a job to do and was thus spared the excruciating boredom that was my lot.

☼ ☼ ☼ ☼ ☼

At this point, John Bowes Griffin's daughter Mary Hannah, using the original draft of the memoirs he wrote before his death as a guide, takes over from Alice Boase.

**Uganda: 1927–36**

In 1926, having obtained a law degree at Trinity College Dublin and been called to the Bar (Inner Temple), Bowes Griffin was in London. There he had his first experience of the forces of law and order when he served as a special constable during the general strike that year, for which he was issued with a police truncheon, which ever afterwards he kept at the side of his bed in case of intruders. He hoped to join the colonial service and was engaged to marry Eva Orrell Walsh, a fellow graduate of Trinity.

In his application to the Colonial Office he deliberately put Uganda last on the list of preferred territories because he wished to avoid all possible charges of nepotism that might stem from the fact that his father, Sir Charles Griffin, was at that time chief justice of Uganda. Bowes did not have the required number of years of experience for direct entry to the colonial legal service, but was accepted for the administrative service on the understanding that two years in that branch, with experience as a magistrate, would enable him to transfer into the legal service. Junior administrative officers had limited jurisdiction in their districts.

Despite his father's presence in Uganda, it was to that territory that he was appointed. First, however, he joined other cadets at Cambridge for a six-months' colonial administrative course. This consisted of lectures designed to prepare recruits for the varied aspects of work ahead of them in criminal law, Mohammedan law, tropical agriculture, phonetics, anthropology, tropical medicine ('which induced the reflection that one was unwise to persevere') and surveying. In the flat landscape of Cambridge and windy cold winter weather, this last was itself a survival test.

Early in May 1927 Bowes put his heavy luggage aboard the *Llandaff Castle* while he went overland to Switzerland to visit his younger sister, Alice, at her finishing school in Fribourg. From there he headed for Marseilles to catch the *Llandaff Castle*, which was *en route* to Uganda, but nearly missed the ship because a railway accident had blocked the line. Fortunately, he got there in time after some adventures; otherwise his career in the colonies might have come to an abrupt end at that point. He was dismayed to discover that his cabin mate was the one man, among the 17 fellow cadets on board, with whom he least wished to share confined quarters. Many of the others remained close friends all their lives, particularly Keith Burner, later a provincial commissioner in Uganda, and Robin Platt who was sadly among those killed when Jewish terrorists blew up the King David Hotel in Jerusalem in 1946.

The ship's next stop was Port Said where he and his friends went ashore and paid the ritual visit to Simon Artz, a shop that stocked sun helmets and other tropical kit. Of course the inevitable Egyptian hawkers came aboard and the gilli-gilli men who amused the passengers with their tricks, and there was the interest of going through the Suez Canal. It was extremely hot in the Red Sea and his cabin was on the wrong side of the ship to get any breeze (the word 'posh' comes from 'port out, starboard home'), so he slept on deck in a chair until driven below to the hot cabin by the hands sluicing the decks at 6 a.m.

A couple of unpleasant days followed while loading coal at Port Sudan. In those primitive days this was done by men running up and down gangplanks, each tipping his sack load of coal into the hold, so clouds of coal dust added to the heat, dirt and discomfort of that port of call.

Aden was the last stop before Mombasa and after visiting it Bowes fervently hoped he would never be posted there. In contrast, the last few days at sea were cooler and more enjoyable; the cadets on board played deck sports and began to feel more optimistic about their future. They sailed into Mombasa at dawn, berthing at Kilindini. Government coast agents met the five cadets bound for Uganda; they organized them, collected their luggage and transferred them to the station in time for the train to Nairobi. Since each came equipped with tropical kit and basic household and safari items, including mosquito boots, spine pads, water filters and camp beds, they all had a good deal of luggage. In London they had been given a small allowance, but not enough to cover what was needed even for bachelor establishments.

It happened to be Empire Day, 24 May 1927, an appropriate date to arrive at the start of their careers.

The train to Nairobi was wood fuelled and driven by Sikhs. Each first-class compartment held four passengers and there were no corridors. The bench seats converted into bunks for the overnight journey to Nairobi, a long slow uphill climb through attractive country with a last view of the sea they would not see again until they went on leave. They stopped for a meal while the bunks were being prepared for the night and hurricane lamps were lit during the halt. A good night's sleep followed and, early next day, as they approached Nairobi, they saw zebra and other game.

Four days in Nairobi followed during which Bowes stayed with the then postmaster general of Kenya, a family friend, at whose house a servant sent from his parents' house in Entebbe awaited him. This was in accordance with the prevailing custom that a servant accompanied a house guest to spare the host's staff additional work. Hatibu was in fact the senior Griffins' head boy and he presented a dignified figure in his long white *kanzu* and red tarboosh. At that time most Baganda men wore these garments, with the long robe tucked up when riding bicycles. Hatibu spoke little English, so the very basic Luganda learnt at Cambridge from a retired Church Missionary Society man was used for the first time in harsh reality.

There was time to explore Nairobi, which was laid out on a grid with wide streets despite there still not being much traffic in those days. Nearly all the buildings were of wood with corrugated iron roofs, from the corners of which the rainwater was drained off into tanks. The buildings were mostly Asian *duka*s, plus some banks and a few offices. The Supreme Court was a large, wide wooden building on stilts and it continued to be used as such until 1935.

On the following Saturday afternoon Bowes rejoined his fellow cadets for the train journey to Kisumu. The train climbed to Limuru and the travellers saw Kikuyu people for the first time, dressed mainly in skins and with ornaments distending the lobes of their ears. They were unsmiling and the general effect of the forest scenery and serious people was eerie in the cold and dark as they stopped at Mau Summit late at night. It was so chilly that sleep proved difficult. The route was downhill now to the railhead at Kisumu on the shore of Lake Victoria, where they embarked on the lake steamer, the *Clement Hill*, for the final leg of the journey. The ship was about 2000 tons and had been in service for many years. Each cadet had a two-berth cabin to himself, which was comfortable and warm, in marked contrast to the previous night on the train. Naturally, they felt excited and rose early to get the first glimpse of the approach to Entebbe as dawn broke. It was misty, but gradually the sun appeared and the landscape was revealed. The word *entebbe* means chair, and the little town set in the centre of low hills, green vegetation and red earth, looked just like the seat and arms of a chair. When the ship drew alongside the jetty the Griffin parents were at the foot of the gangway to meet their son. (Presumably, there were also people there to meet the other cadets!) Bowes was taken to the chief justice's house. It was built on the curving main road overlooking a sloping hill and nine-hole golf course, and had an excellent view of Lake Victoria. In his own words:

> The house, an old one with a new complete bedroom and bathroom wing added, was charmingly arranged. My mother always had a genius for home making and in the management of African staff, despite little command of Luganda or the brand of Swahili (the coast language) used in Uganda. All the staff were fond of her and showed it in their work.

There is a photograph showing no less than ten servants to sustain their household. It should be remembered that in

1927 in Entebbe, and Uganda generally, there was no electricity, piped water, waterborne sanitation or an inch of tarmac. This meant that a large staff was necessary to run European households and it was normal at that time to have a head boy, a cook, a kitchen boy (*toto jikoni*), houseboys and a *dhobi* to do the laundry as well as garden (*shamba*) boys. The term 'boy' was not regarded as politically incorrect then!

Bowes had expected to see his parents only briefly prior to being posted, like his fellow cadets, to Kampala for an introductory few weeks in the district commissioner's office before being sent off to other districts away from the two main centres of Entebbe and Kampala. However, he was told that he was to remain in Entebbe to work in the crown law office as assistant to the attorney general. Indeed, the office was within easy walking distance of his parents' house, at one end of the same building in which his father sat as chief justice of the high court – in other words, the very situation both father and son had hoped to avoid. In fact, a real need existed for a qualified lawyer as a prosecutor because both the attorney general and the crown counsel were away on leave and the senior magistrate was acting as attorney general. The urgent need for more legally qualified staff overrode the lack of previous experience, which had earlier, in London, been the reason for his initial recruitment into the administration. To add to the problem, there were also financial constraints on employing more staff, so those who decided these matters in Entebbe felt that the 'bird in the hand' should be diverted from the administrative side, despite his father's position so close to him in the same office building.

So, on the morning after his arrival in Entebbe, Bowes duly reported to the acting attorney general. The crown law office, a wing of the high court building, consisted of three rooms: one for the attorney general, a second to be used by 'the new boy', and a third where two Goanese clerks worked. Despite being Portuguese citizens, these Portuguese Asians were the mainstay of all the East African civil service offices. They efficiently performed all clerical and secretarial duties at a time when few local people had attained a high enough standard of education to fill such posts, as they did of course in later years.

The acting attorney general, who was about 45 years old, gave his new underling a warm welcome, a huge pile of secretariat minute papers and the files of a murder case in which Bowes was to prosecute later that week.

The attorney general in every colony was the government's chief legal advisor and the second most senior ex-officio member of the Executive Council (the chief secretary being the first, immediately under the governor). He was also in the Legislative Council, a larger body – the Executive Council being, as it were, the local Cabinet while the Legislative Council was a mini-parliament. In 1927 it only had official and European members, but this changed with the march towards independence many years later. The attorney general's office also drafted and introduced legislation to be enacted by the Legislative Council. The department's other responsibility was to negotiate agreements between the government and local rulers in Buganda, Bunyoro, Toro and Ankole.

Thus, Bowes had a swift introduction to legal work. He had only a few days to study the case for the prosecution in the murder trial, appearing bewigged and gowned for the first time in a high court. At that time Uganda's laws were based on the Indian penal code, which a Legislative Council ordinance had made applicable to Uganda. This code was used until 1930. The trial was by a judge with three or more assessors who were of the same tribe and language as the accused. The judge was not bound by the assessors' opinions; their main function was as a check on the inter-preters and witnesses. Bowes wrote of this trial: 'As I remember, I got through the prosecution and my first case ever quite adequately', but he does not actually say what the verdict was.

Ten days later he had to appear for the crown in sessions in the Eastern Province. So he went to Jinja where the Nile flowed out of Lake Victoria and where the Owen Falls Dam now stands. With no road bridge at that time it was necessary to use the ferry between the Buganda and Busoga shores. Jinja, still a very small town, was the provincial headquarters and boasted a primitive hotel in which the bedrooms were African-style huts around a central dining room and reception area.

The sessions took about a fortnight, with manslaughter and murder cases being dealt with first. Many of these stemmed from drunken brawls at beer parties. Any conviction involving a death penalty went on appeal to the East African court of appeal in Nairobi, where the chief justices of each of the territories – Kenya, Uganda, Tanganyika and Zanzibar – sat. During the Eastern Province sessions the court also sat at Mbale and Soroti, involving long drives over dirt roads in cars that at that time only had hoods and side curtains and thus were anything but dust and rainproof. Accommodation was in rest houses, so these journeys gave Bowes his first experience in adult life of African safaris. He found them not very much more comfortable or sophisticated than his childhood memories of them had been in Nyasaland 20 years before.

On his return to Entebbe he began to settle down more and was able to buy a Morris Cowley from a retiring missionary; this car was a great success and served him well for the next few years. He became more familiar with the work and enjoyed it, as well as the customary colonial practice of finishing work in time for tennis before the sudden tropical nightfall. He was able to apply for permission to marry when he had completed his first six-months' service, and it was granted. The crown counsel, for whom he had been acting, returned from leave and Bowes finally did the administrative training course that he should have done on first arrival. He had completed this by late November when his fiancée, Eva Walsh, arrived for their marriage.

As already described, it so happened that Alice Griffin, Bowes's younger sister, had just left school, so the two of them travelled out together, sharing a cabin and being carefully chaperoned by an older married woman who, with her husband, were friends of Alice's parents. There was no adventurous and enterprising solo backpacking for young ladies in 1927.

Alice had experienced life in Africa as a small child, but for Eva it was all a new experience as until then she had only travelled in Europe. It must have been exciting and perhaps a bit daunting to be on board the lake steamer as it arrived at Entebbe with her fiancé, his parents, his other sister Kathleen (Kits) and her husband and daughter Aileen (on leave from India) on the quay awaiting them. The Griffins of course made all the wedding preparations because Eva's family were at home in Dublin. The couple were married on 8 December 1927 in the White Fathers' Catholic church in Entebbe, a dried mud and wood building with a corrugated tin roof supported by crudely cut tree trunks. The Dutch priest, Father Laane, whose command of English was graphic rather than accurate, had assured the bride that the altar boys would decorate the church 'with garlands of vegetables'. It was quite a relief then to find the pillars swathed only in frangipani, bougainvillaea, palm leaves and papyrus fronds!

The wedding reception was held in the senior Griffin's (chief justice's) garden. Alice was Eva's bridesmaid and Bowes's brother-in-law, 'Mullano' (Charles Mullan), was his best man. By Uganda standards it was the social event of the year and guests included the Kabaka of Buganda, along with his *katikiro*, *omulamazi* and *omwanika*. The newly-weds set off for their honeymoon in their recently acquired Morris – of course with one servant as custom required – to a coffee estate called Bwavu. It was situated between Kampala and Jinja, about 45 miles from Entebbe, and had kindly been lent to them by its owner Captain Maxted, known as 'the Squire of Bwavu'. Unlike Kenya, it was rare in Uganda to have freehold tenure and there were not many settlers, so he was exceptional and they spent a delightful week in his comfortably furnished, well-established house with a beautiful garden and well-trained staff.

Bowes's fellow cadets had jokingly accused him of pulling strings to get his pleasant six months in Entebbe on first arrival. Now, however, the regular legal officials had returned from leave and he had to fulfil the probationary period of administrative work in a district away from the capital. His friends forecast 'Soroti for you', naming the least popular posting, and Soroti it proved to be.

Teso district was known as an unhealthy area and its main centre, where the district commissioner was stationed, was at Soroti. When the Griffins set off they knew that it was not at that time a happy place. The few Europeans already there were involved in petty feuding; there had been a long drought; and then, just as the vegetation and crops had begun to grow again, they were hit by a swarm of locusts, so the people were threatened by famine.

Shortly after Christmas 1927, their household equipment and heavy luggage was loaded onto a lorry and the driver, joined by a newly recruited cook called Munganda, set off for Soroti. The Griffins left Entebbe in their Morris Cowley with Yusefu Kigongo, the golf clubs and rifle, plus other luggage squashed into the dickey seat at the back. Their first stop was Jinja, the provincial headquarters, to allow Bowes to touch his hat to his new superior, the provincial commissioner. After a couple of days there, they set off for Tororo to spend one night with their great friend, Keith Burner, a fellow cadet. They left Jinja rather late in the day and it was already dark when they drove up the hill to the government quarters. Eva was driving and in the beam of the headlights

156

a leopard suddenly appeared, was dazzled momentarily, but then luckily vanished.

They accomplished the last stretch of the journey to Soroti the following day and arrived, hot and dusty, at lunch time. The district commissioner, who was to be Bowes's immediate superior, was just going into his house to eat, but he did not invite them to join him!

Despite this tepid welcome they soon settled into their allotted bungalow. In his original draft Bowes pays tribute to his young wife's cheerful adaptation to the totally strange lifestyle and to how quickly she made the house as comfortable and well run as circumstances permitted, with the servants working as a team. Meanwhile, Bowes started work wearing the then obligatory khaki administration uniform with brass buttons, each with Uganda's emblem of a golden crested crane, and of course a pith helmet.

The office staff consisted of the district commissioner, another assistant district officer in addition to Bowes, a doctor, a Public Works Department foreman, and one Indian and two Goan clerks. The three clerks were always helpful and amiable, the other European officials less so. The people of Teso were Nilotic, not Bantu, so had their own language, which was a further complication.

On a camping safari covering three parts of the district and lasting three weeks, Eva had a very bad attack of malaria and a mission doctor and his wife very kindly looked after her at a leper hospital. For the rest of their time in Soroti, Bowes remained based at the station in charge of distributing millet to alleviate the famine conditions. He went out each day to different distribution centres and, when the rain came at last, he controlled the supplies of food, including maize flour, until there was a harvest once more.

Each evening they solemnly changed for dinner. Bowes would wear an old pair of evening trousers, a white evening shirt, a black tie and a cummerbund. His bride would choose between her wedding gown, on the grounds that she might as well get a bit more wear out of it, or one of her simpler 1920s flapper style dresses. Being a fire hazard, the kitchen was in a separate building, so the food had to be carried across to the house. Although the house was wired against mosquitoes in the normal manner, each time the back door was opened, the waiting mosquitoes would take advantage and nip in for their chance of a meal. Eva found that her bare arms and legs – at least between the hem of her 1920s short skirt and the top of her mosquito boots – were regularly bitten. Her solution to this problem was to make 'bishop's sleeves', which she pinned to her shoulder seams and held at the wrist with elastic, and a bag from a doubled sheet into which she inserted herself to protect her bottom half. When dinner was served she would move from the sitting room to the table as though competing in a sack race!

After ten months they left Soroti with no regrets, glad that the authorities had curtailed Bowes's probationary period as a cadet and now confirmed his appointment as a colonial legal officer. His new position was acting registrar of the high court in Entebbe. Thus, they were in more civilized surroundings when their elder daughter Daphne Mary was born in the hospital at Nakasero, Kampala, on 15 November 1928. In 1929 Bowes was promoted to registrar of the high court.

At the end of 1930, while Bowes' father Sir Charles Griffin was still chief justice, the fine new high court building was opened in Kampala and both the senior and junior Griffin households moved there from Entebbe to be near the new premises. Also in 1930 the younger branch of the family went on home leave. There was still no railway from Kampala, so their departure was from Entebbe across Lake Victoria to Kisumu on the *Clement Hill*. There were only two other passengers and all dined together at the captain's table. The other two were Mr and Mrs Neville Chamberlain who did not address a single word to anyone throughout dinner or for the rest of the journey. Perhaps *mal de mer* accounted for their aloofness because the lake that night was very stormy. Thereafter, the voyage back to Europe and their leave on the whole were enjoyable, concluding with a six-weeks return journey via the west coast, round the Cape and up the east coast to Mombasa on the *Llanstephan Castle*. They then drove across Kenya and back to Uganda in their new car, an Austin Twelve 'special colonial model', which they had collected from the factory in England. On this leave also Bowes had his first experience of traffic lights and, having never heard of them before, he was momentarily puzzled by the pretty changing colours.

The years from 1931 to 1936 were spent happily partly in Kampala and partly in Entebbe. At first Bowes was registrar of the high court, but later he was given the task of producing the laws of Uganda – to replace the Indian penal code as adapted for Uganda that had been used up until then. His personal set of these laws is now in the School of Oriental and African Studies library in London. He also acted as crown counsel for part of this time and 'acting' solicitor general and 'acting' attorney general when the substantive officials were on leave. Thus, by 1935/6 he had nine years of varied administrative and legal experience to his credit.

It should be explained here that, whereas officials in the administration tended to stay in the countries where they had acquired local experience and knew the languages and were promoted within that frame, those in the much smaller colonial legal service had to move territories in order to rise to more illustrious heights. There were, for example, fewer senior judicial posts than there were jobs as provincial commissioners, chief secretaries or governors. Although the Griffins were very happy in Uganda, Bowes was advised that if he wanted promotion he should accept a post offered to him in 1936 as attorney general of the Bahamas, despite the very real disadvantage of a lower salary, no housing and no fares paid. The Bahamas were a much poorer colony than Uganda where in any case his salary was scarcely princely, especially during the depression years of the late 1920s and early 1930s when all officials in Uganda had their salaries arbitrarily reduced to help the government cope with the shortage of funds. His salary in the Bahamas would be £800 per annum. After much thought Bowes accepted the position, having first explained to his bank manager in London that his future prospects depended on taking the job – in those days one had a working relationship with this mighty person – whereupon it was agreed that he could operate an overdraft to cover the shortfall caused by having to pay transatlantic fares for himself, Eva and Daphne, and rent for a house in Nassau. In case there should be any idea that 'vile imperialists' made their fortunes in the colonies, it should be added that the overdraft started in 1936 still haunted the Griffins until the late 1940s when his salary in Hong Kong was at last high enough to live on with care and clear the debt.

## The Bahamas: 1936–39

To economize, the family took second-class passages on board the *Reina del Pacifico* to travel to Nassau, the capital of the Bahamas on New Providence Island. Because of its inability to negotiate Atlantic storms with any degree of comfort, the ship was nicknamed the *Rolly Reina* and the Pacific Steam Navigation Company, the shipping company to which it belonged, was referred to as the 'Passengers Shall Not Complain' Line. Fellow sufferers included Spaniards heading for Chile and Peru to avoid the Spanish civil war then threatening.

The Bahamas consists of a large number of not very fertile islands. At that time Nassau boasted electricity, tarred roads and proper sanitation, so in those respects at least it was an improvement on Entebbe. But the Griffins' first impressions were not very cheering and they wondered whether their move had been a wise one. They had great difficulty finding suitable and affordable housing; there was no proper school for Daphne, then aged nearly eight; and they had arrived at the beginning of the hurricane season. This marks the start of the long, hot, humid and sandfly-ridden summer of the West Indies, which lasts nearly eight months, in contrast with the months between November and March each year when the climate is delightful.

The marked difference in the two seasons had one small advantage, namely that during the unpleasant months the Bahamians were prepared to let their houses at slightly lower rents to people like the Griffins and other expatriate officials. But they were required to move out in the fashionable cooler months so that the locals could charge even higher rents to wealthy visiting Americans. For two years the Griffins had fairly decent houses during the humid season and then ones no one else wanted to rent for the rest of the time. One fellow official's solution to the housing problem caused comment when he decided to rent from a local landlord all year round, but move with his family into the servants' quarters during the tourist months while he sublet the main house to visiting Americans.

An end to this very unsatisfactory situation came in their final year when a few pleasant houses were built for expatriate officials and the family greatly enjoyed living in a delightful new home with direct access to an attractive beach, swimming straight from their own garden steps. In every other respect there was no improvement; the cost of living was high and there was still no schooling for Daphne, who thus was sent to England at a very young age to join her cousins, Aileen and Pamela Mullan, at St Mary's Convent in Ascot.

Whoever encouraged Bowes to accept the job in the Bahamas because it would widen his experience and extend the range of his work had given him good advice. In the three-and-a-half years in the islands he not only served as attorney general but also acted as chief justice for a brief period and twice as acting governor. Once, while bewigged and gowned as chief justice at the hottest time of the year he said he had been taught a lesson about displaying irritation or impatience from the bench. He told a mumbling Bahamian witness to speak up and give the court his name loudly and clearly, adding that if his name were worth giving it were worth giving well. Then, much to the amusement of the packed courtroom, the witness readily and loudly responded, 'My name is Griffin, the same as yours.'

In his appointed capacity as attorney general, Bowes was the only legally qualified civil servant apart from the chief justice. He therefore covered every aspect of official work: advisory, legal draughtsmanship, criminal prosecutions, contracts, agreements and conveyancing, with the help of only two clerk typists. As in Uganda, the governor worked through an executive council (with three official and some unofficial members) and a legislative council, on both of which Bowes served. These councils controlled government expenditure and directed all public services, including public works, health and the port authority.

In addition to his normal responsibilities, soon after his arrival Bowes was made chairman of the new Bahamas Development Board, which was concerned with attempts to improve the local economy. In the past some employment had come from collecting and exporting sponges from the coral reefs, but a disease that killed all the sponges, in what nowadays would be called an ecological disaster, had ended that source of income for the many sponge fishermen. During the years of prohibition in the United States, prosperity had come in a small way to the islands from tourists in search of a drink and from illicit bootlegging, so the end of this unpopular US policy was another blow to Bahamian enterprise. The Development Board was set up to encourage tourism and Bowes was sent to New York to contact US travel agencies, advertising firms and shipping companies. This commercial work was very different from his usual legal concerns and he found it an exciting and stimulating experience. These small beginnings were the foundations on which the huge modern tourist industry that has brought such prosperity to the Bahamas was built, while the visits to New York were a revelation after the rural simplicity of Uganda and the islands.

Off duty Bowes and his family, including Mary who was born in 1937, particularly enjoyed the beaches and swimming. Daphne was able to join them part of the time but her schooling in England made long separations inevitable. She crossed the Atlantic several times, once with her Griffin grandparents who came out on a visit from their retirement home in Guernsey. In July 1939 Eva went home to be with Daphne for her summer holidays, leaving Mary in the care of Bowes and her Turks Islander nanny, Pearl. During that holiday Eva and Daphne were staying with the family in Guernsey as the outbreak of war loomed. Fortunately, they were able to secure passages on the SS *Antonia* to cross the Atlantic and they arrived in Montreal on 3 September 1939, the day war broke out and also the date on which a German submarine sank a Cunard sister ship, the SS *Athenia*. They travelled from Canada to New York by train and from there by seaplane to Nassau, which at that time still had no airfield. Thus, the family was more fortunate than many in that it was possible to spend the war years together. This period was not, however, to be spent entirely in Nassau because in October 1939 Bowes accepted a new appointment as solicitor general in Palestine.

## Palestine: 1940–46

Seen off by many good friends, on 1 December 1939 the Griffin family left Nassau by ship for New York. There, in an old-style three-storey town house dwarfed by surrounding skyscrapers, they stayed for a week with the Nason family in East Forty-Second Street. From New York, they had obtained passages on an American ship, *The Excalibur*. To emphasize America's neutrality and, consequently, as a protection against attacks from German submarines in the Atlantic, stars and stripes were clearly painted on its hull, the ship was well illuminated at night and it carried the American flag. While at sea Bowes and Eva followed the radio broadcasts about the Battle of the River Plate with special interest because they had got to know the officers on board HMS *Exeter* (which took part in the battle) when the ship had been 'showing the flag' in the Bahamas during King George VI's coronation celebrations. *The Excalibur*'s American registration did not, however, prevent long delays in Gibraltar, Genoa and Alexandria as the ship's holds and documents were being examined for any contraband cargo that might flout its neutrality. On 10 January 1940 it arrived at Haifa on a particularly cold day. Luckily, the Griffins had been able to buy warm clothing during their few days in New York, but the yeomanry being discharged with their horses from a troopship tied up to the same quay were all wearing khaki drill summer uniforms with pith helmets.

From Haifa, where they were met, the four Griffins drove to Jerusalem and, on the Ramallah Road as the car emerged from the surrounding hills, to an unforgettable first view of the Old City in winter sunshine. Bowes was about to embark on work and to experience quite different problems in a third continent within four years, but it was the significance of being in Jerusalem that was uppermost in his thoughts that day.

A snippet of news in the *Palestine Post* that January read, without punctuation: 'Mr J. B. Griffin named new Solicitor General 3000 British gas masks arrive in Haifa'!

First impressions of life in Jerusalem were based on a stay of several weeks in the American Colony – a hotel some

American missionaries had founded many years before – while the Griffins house hunted, for no official quarters were provided. They found a large, modern flat in a block of four in Katamon, a suburb of Jerusalem within fairly easy reach of the city centre. The flat was on the ground floor with small walled gardens back and front – anything but luxuriant – and a large, useful cellar storage area, a boiler room for the central heating and a garage. It had three bedrooms and three reception rooms, but one of these was always given over to the succession of maids of varying nationalities and faiths who marched in and out of our domestic lives: English, Arab (Muslim and Christian), Armenian and Jewish (German, Polish and Russian). The best of these were two middle-aged Christian Arab sisters called Marie and Katrine. Having been brought up in an orphanage run by French nuns, they spoke a Levantine type of French that became the medium of communication between them and Eva and that both Daphne and Mary picked up. They were an awkward, quarrelsome pair, always at odds with each other and not easy to manage. Bowes gave them the nicknames of 'Giraud' and 'de Gaulle', notorious then for the arguments they had after the fall of France in 1940 and during the North African campaigns. Each evening when they had finished work and retired to their shared room next door to the family sitting room, a strange rasping noise could be heard, followed by a silence, and then an argument would break out that always seemed to be about money. The angry stage whispers could easily be overheard and when Bowes eventually tackled them about the disturbance each night, he was alarmed to learn that a suitcase they kept under one bed contained their life savings. The next morning they were firmly frog-marched to the bank to deposit their hoard.

Bowes was able to buy a second-hand Austin 10. However, when petrol rationing was brought in the flat was well-placed for the fleet of shaky old buses that linked Katamon, via the Greek Colony and the German Colony (other suburbs), to the area near the King David Hotel and to the centre of modern Jerusalem and the Jaffa Road, ending at the Jaffa Gate into the Old City.

Throughout the time of the British Mandate of Palestine it had never been possible for financial reasons to provide government departments with purpose-built premises. They operated for the most part from rented offices, often shared with other organizations and so impossible to control from a security point of view. Bowes was aware of the situation and had alerted the authorities to the potential hazard, but nothing could be done during the war. As events turned out, with the unleashing of Jewish nationalism when the war ended and the fear of Hitler was removed, his anxieties turned out to have been justified. In the meanwhile, because a building at the Damascus Gate that had attracted Arab snipers during the troubles in the 1930s needed to be vacated, a couple of years earlier the government had taken over a wing of the King David Hotel to provide office accommodation for the army's Palestine headquarters, the secretariat and the legal department.

The staff of the legal department included the attorney general, William Fitzgerald, Bowes as solicitor general, legal draughtsmen, and crown counsel and government advocates, both Jewish and Arab. Four out of six expatriate officials in the office were of Irish origin, as were many others in the legal service in the colonies. It was a happy department and the work, of which there was always a great deal, was interesting, with the additional special problems arising from the age-old divisions, conflicts and jealousies of the various religious bodies and factions in that contentious 'Holy Land'. Bowes recalled that he arrived on the first morning in his new office to find it was a corner room of the second floor of the King David Hotel, with a view from one window over the Kedron Valley to the Old City and from another of a landscape stretching to the Moab mountains.

The topmost file on his desk was referred for advice on the question of the repair, and its cost, of the chapel of Saint Helena in the Holy Sepulchre. Greek Orthodox Church members were strident in their demand to be allowed to pay the cost of the work. The other Christian sects or churches were equally insistent that the Greeks should not be allowed to pay in whole or part because to do so would (or might) increase their rights in the church of the Holy Sepulchre. This was his introduction to the typically thorny problems of his new job. It was clear that the dispute could only be resolved by insisting on maintaining the status quo that had evolved and been enforced during the years of the Turkish occupation of the country. Bowes therefore advised that the government should effect and pay for the repairs to Saint Helena's chapel, thus avoiding an unedifying quarrel among the various Christian Churches.

The family settled into the flat and were fortunately able to buy furniture from people who were about to leave. Daphne started at the Sisters of Sion's English language school in Katamon, but slept along with the other boarders in the Ecce Homo Convent in the Via Dolorosa, to and from which they travelled in an old brown school bus each day. A year or so later Mary joined the kindergarten as a day pupil.

Petrol rationing had not yet been imposed and in those early months of the war it was possible to explore the country, visiting Bethlehem only a few miles from Jerusalem and many other significant places. They also had the occasional trip to the beach at Jaffa and picnics in the Palestinian countryside, especially attractive when the wild flowers were out after the winter rain but dry and stony in the long weeks of the summer.

Life became more serious once Italy entered the war and the desert campaign began. Because there were attacks on shipping in the Mediterranean all supplies and reinforcements for Palestine and Egypt had to be sent on the longer sea route via the Cape and Suez Canal before continuing by rail to Palestine, so food rationing and other steps were of course necessary. All Italian and German nationals were interned and a department, namely the Custodian of Enemy Property, was especially set up to administer their property and business affairs. Eva worked for this body, finding it interesting and therefore a satisfying outlet for her considerable abilities. This was the only time she was able to work because, throughout most of Bowes's career, her own legal training could not be used professionally for fear of a conflict of interests with his work.

Bowes, among other things, became chairman of a review committee dealing with appeals from 'aliens'. The fall of France in 1940 had implications for the administration of Syria and Lebanon, which France had been governing under a League of Nations Mandate similar to Britain's in Palestine. Now, with the Vichy France government in control, there was a danger to British people in the adjacent territory; Bowes was one of the officials who tried to help a Free French group that had gathered in Jerusalem set up a pro-Allies civil administration. In the event, no civil government was possible and the two countries were under Free French military control until the war ended and the United Nations gave them their independence. When the British and Free French jointly entered Beirut, the Germans, Italians and Vichy French had left so precipitately that their kit was still in their rooms, and their beds were unmade because the staff had also vanished from the hotels and houses they had occupied.

With fears of an attack from Vichy-controlled Syria and Lebanon from one direction and of the desert campaign endangering Palestine and Egypt from another, all civil servants and British civilians in Jerusalem joined the Palestine volunteer force, which was attached to the army's Palestine command. Bowes belonged to the No. 1 Jerusalem company and reached the rank of corporal. They paraded and trained twice a week at Allenby barracks in Jerusalem and on a musketry range in the countryside nearby. On an extremely cold night exercise, one elderly volunteer in this particular Dad's Army was heard to ask whether there was such a thing as triple pneumonia! Perhaps fortunately, they were not called upon to engage in serious action, but their responsibilities included anti-aircraft duty on the roof of the King David Hotel, on which there were two Lewis guns. Because of its size and prominent position, the hotel was conspicuous in Jerusalem, but luckily there was only one occasion when aircraft flew nearby and that was when the Vichy French dropped leaflets before their above-mentioned departure. Although Haifa suffered several raids, with its oil storage tanks being an inevitable target, there was an unspoken agreement that Jerusalem would never be bombed.

Every aspect of Bowes's work was to do with balancing the interests of the rival communities. Thus, while many of the 'aliens' whose cases he reviewed were Jews of German nationality, at the same time he was a member of another committee that aimed to establish an effective Arab village administration as a substitute for the tattered remnants of what had been the Turkish regime before the Mandate began. The chairman of this committee was a man called Maurice Bailey, but he died soon afterwards while he was district commissioner of Jerusalem. He had originally come to Palestine with Allenby during the First World War and his long experience and great knowledge of the country were invaluable. With the other members of this committee, Bowes spent many weekends travelling throughout Palestine, but in the end the recommendations for the Arab villages they made in their report could not be applied because of the inevitable conflict with other communities. The proposals and draft legislation contained in the report, however, later formed a basis for action in Malaya when another former committee member, Sir Donald McGillivray, 'borrowed' the framework to adapt for use there.

In a rather different vein, Bowes chaired a commission set up to examine the finances and grievances of employees of the Tel Aviv municipality. The inquiry threw light on the special difficulties that confronted an important municipal council whose individually competent members were in conflict. They were all Jews but at that time they were also British, or German, or Polish, or Russian, or American – a veritable Tower of Babel. They still needed time to weld together, as happened with new generations and the firm establishment of Hebrew as the official language in Israel.

The period between mid-1940 and October 1942, when the Allies were victorious at El Alamein, saw Palestine as ever more vulnerable, especially after the Germans took control of Greece and Crete. The Palestine government decided to offer expatriate women and children the chance to evacuate to South Africa via the Suez Canal. The plan was that they should board the ship at Suez. When this was proposed at a meeting, Bowes pointed out that the Italians were regularly bombing Suez and suggested that the women and children should travel further by train and embark at Port Sudan, but this was considered impractical. The Griffins had decided to keep their family together, so Eva, Daphne and Mary were not among those aboard the SS *Georgic* when it was bombed, with many tragic fatalities and badly burnt casualties. Thereafter, there was no further suggestion of evacuations.

Tensions in Palestine rose as Hitler's army pushed into Russia, renewing the fear of attack through Turkey and the danger to oil pipelines. Bowes at this time was involved in negotiations with Egypt over the claims for shipping and transport that Palestine had requisitioned from Egypt and used in the evacuation of Crete, as well as over the debts that these incurred. On his way to Egypt for discussions with the marine ministry at Port Said, he and the controller of customs, J. W. Gregory, drove across the Sinai desert in a sandstorm, which was a scary experience for them all. (Eva accompanied them, but it proved to be more of an ordeal than a holiday break.)

Ever since Hitler and the Nazis first began to implement their appalling 'solution' to the Jewish question, desperate refugees had tried to enter Palestine. Small, dangerously overloaded and barely seaworthy ships would run aground on the beaches of Palestine; their passengers would attempt to land and 'disappear', but many were captured and held as illegal immigrants. Arab sensibilities had to be taken into account, for it was essential to avoid a recurrence of the armed revolts that Arab rage at Jewish immigration had caused in the 1930s. With the security of the pipelines and peace in Palestine being crucial given that the oil wells in the Middle East were vital to the war effort, a decision was made to move the hordes of illegal immigrants out of Palestine to Mauritius, and to readdress the problem at the end of the war. An old French liner, the *Patria*, which had been in the port in Haifa when France fell, was requisitioned for the purpose. Hundreds of people were on board preparatory to sailing under the charge of British Palestine police officers when either one or more bombs placed in the ship exploded. The ship turned on its side and sank in Haifa harbour, and many passengers died. In the judicial inquiry that followed, Bowes appeared for the Palestine government. The Jews who placed the bombs on board had hoped that the *Patria* would sink slowly and remain upright in shallow water, thus allowing the passengers to escape and thereafter be allowed to remain in Palestine. Their plan went terribly wrong. The Jews had resorted to desperate measures while the British were trying to maintain their control and protect Arab concerns. As always, no solution was fair to everyone, which Bowes and his colleagues in the Mandate government found dispiriting. There was no prospect of a peaceful outcome, no matter how much effort was made by men of great integrity in an honest government. At best, they were simply holding the fires in check. Both Arabs and Jews were too intransigent ever to agree; their interests were irreconcilable and all concerned were prejudiced. The best that conscientious civil servants could do was to attempt to govern fairly. One of Bowes's colleagues described this as ploughing sand.

Overwork inevitably had its effect and for many years Bowes suffered from duodenal ulcers, not helped by wartime food rationing, which made following a strict diet very difficult. Rest was impossible and, as the war drew to its close, the Jewish terrorists ended their unofficial amnesty – it had not been in their interest to impede the war effort against Hitler – and began to cause trouble once more. On the advice of his doctor, which in retrospect he said was exceedingly foolish, in 1944 Bowes flew to wartime Britain for a one-month leave. As flying bombs were landing on London at that time, it was anything but the rest cure he desired, but he did manage to see his parents who had been evacuated from Guernsey to more peaceful Cheltenham. His return flight to Egypt was delayed at the RAF airfield from which they were to leave by the departure of aircraft and gliders heading for Arnhem. On arrival in Egypt Bowes headed for Alexandria where his family awaited him; they had been attempting to have a seaside holiday there because they could not all get passages to England, which had been granted exceptionally to Bowes because of his health.

Here it should be recorded that Daphne had passed her higher certificate at an exceptionally early age. She in fact took the exam three times and might well have passed it sooner had the first two sets of papers not been lost when each of the ships carrying them to London for marking were sunk in the Mediterranean. At 16 she was thus in an awkward situation. The nuns could not provide her with further education, she was too young to join the war effort and going to university in England was not possible while the war lasted. Fortunately, among the Griffins' friends in

Jerusalem there were scholars who were willing to give her private tutorials and she benefited greatly from these for the next 18 months. Otherwise, she was in limbo, neither young enough nor old enough for anything; it must have been a difficult time for her. Her parents were immensely proud of her academic and career achievements, then and later.

In 1945 VE and VJ days were duly celebrated in Jerusalem with official military parades; those civil servants who were entitled to do so wore their smart white colonial service uniforms complete with white pith helmets and swords – these were the last occasions on which Bowes wore his. Thereafter, for official celebrations such as the King's or Queen's Birthday, most civil servants wore morning dress, ordinary suits or judicial robes, apart from governors who continued to appear in full panoply with feathers in their hats. Uniforms were regarded as an unnecessary extravagance in the austere postwar years, especially as the colonial era was coming to an end. The victories over Germany and Japan had left a legacy of damage and shortages, which inevitably affected everyone for years afterwards. Apart from the rationing of food and clothes, there were restrictions on travel because of the loss of ships during the war. This meant that home leaves were long overdue and the Griffins had to wait until March 1946 for their turn to come. They travelled on a very small Norwegian cargo vessel that took only eight passengers and was loaded with the first shipment of oranges (without refrigeration) from Palestine to Ireland after the war. It was a memorably rough voyage, made worse by the smell of rotting fruit! Their relations standing on the quayside in Dublin were all dressed in black: a telegram announcing the death of Eva's stepfather had failed to reach the ship and her mother was seriously ill. Their time in Ireland was therefore sad and anxious, but it was also a chance, after eight years without a proper break, to re-establish contact with family and friends and to enjoy a European spring and early summer. From Ireland the family crossed to England to see the Griffin parents in Cheltenham.

The general advice at this point was that Daphne would stand a better chance of obtaining a place at a university if she applied from a school, for ex-servicewomen were being given priority among adults and school-leavers were being considered before other young adults who were not just out of uniform. So Daphne went back to being a schoolgirl and she and Mary both went to the Sisters of Sion convent at Worthing – in Mary's case just for one term – giving Eva a chance to spend more time in Dublin during her mother's illness. The plan worked well and in due course Daphne went to Bedford College, London, where she read history, obtained her degree and made many lifelong friends.

In April, the Colonial Office offered Bowes the post of Attorney General in Hong Kong. However, at the time his health continued to be poor so, on his doctor's advice and following discussions with the Colonial Office, the offer was shelved for the time being.

Hong Kong, as it happened, was still being administered by the military as it had been since the defeat of the Japanese occupiers. Luckily, with a few months of rest his health improved and, in early July 1946, Bowes, Eva and Mary sailed from Liverpool on the SS *Javanese Prince* to return to Palestine.

They were lucky once again to get three passages together, for travel was still strictly controlled, especially for dependants. The ship had docked in Alexandria on 22 July when news came of an atrocious terrorist attack on the wing of the King David Hotel housing the government offices.

There had been many casualties and great loss of life among Bowes's colleagues and friends, including Bernard Bourdillon, George Farley and Robin Platt. The perpetrators of this horrendous crime were from the Jewish terrorist group Irgun led by Menachem Begin, later to become prime

174

minister of Israel.[7] Bowes described what he saw in the extract that follows:

> With Eva's full agreement, I left the ship and took the train to Cairo and Port Said, thence by Palestine Railway to Jerusalem, which I reached 24 hours after the outrage. I was met by our chief clerk and went to the King David Hotel ... where there was a huge pile of debris from what had been the whole corner of the building that had been destroyed. Beneath that cairn were 91 soldiers, civil servants, men and women, British, Arab and Jewish, many of them close friends and colleagues. The legal department casualties were six in number, five Jewish and one Arab. Troops were at work in a rescue attempt and continued for some days to remove the bodies of the victims of an outrage that at that time shocked even the war-hardened world beyond Jerusalem. For us in the city the state of shock was of course greatest. In retrospect it is remarkable that reaction among the British was so restrained and disciplined.

The days that followed were occupied with identifying the bodies and holding the funerals of the victims. Those who had survived moved to new rooms in the unaffected wings of the hotel, all of which had now been requisitioned for government and army use. Security was greatly, if belatedly, intensified; the work went on and a measure of routine was restored.

The destruction of the King David was only one of many incidents in the years between the end of the war and the last days of the mandate in 1948. When the ship at last

---

7. By a curious coincidence, Menachem Begin, for whom Bowes always had the greatest contempt, died on 2 February 1992, the same day as John Bowes Griffin himself.

docked at Haifa, and Eva and Mary were able to rejoin Bowes in Jerusalem, they found the city in a state of high alert. Barbed wire and armed guards surrounded all possible terrorist targets and the Griffins' flat was guarded day and night, though it is doubtful how effective one solitary Arab policeman could have been. There were curfews and controls in place and the atmosphere was tense. Many expatriates sent their wives and children home for safety. There were numerous hoax telephone calls of bomb warnings so that offices had to be evacuated and searched, causing much disruption to work. A regular drill was introduced in government offices to cope with such emergencies. The staff on each floor of the building would leave the premises in reverse order of seniority, with the most senior member being charged with the duty of stowing out of sight all secret and confidential files before joining the rest of the civil servants in the garden or street below. They would then wait for the bomb disposal men to complete their search and declare the building safe – until the next time.

During these weeks the problem of illegal immigration had become acute. RAF coastal patrols and the navy would spot numerous ships and small boats laden with Jewish refugees from Europe who had somehow escaped the Holocaust, and the police would seize them when they attempted to land their passengers. The immigrants were held in detention subject to the quota allowed into Palestine in an attempt not to exasperate the Arabs further. This resulted in a stream of habeas corpus petitions in the Supreme Court in which Bowes appeared for the government, thus making him a prime target for the terrorists. It was no longer safe for him to live in the flat in Katamon, so he and his family packed up and moved, along with many other officials and their families, into the well-guarded German Hospice surrounded by a barbed wire fence. Their furniture and personal belongings had been packed up ready to be sent to Hong Kong, for

Bowes's appointment as attorney general, mooted earlier that year, had by then been finalized, the more urgently because he was known to be in danger of assassination. When the packing cases were ready for collection, Bowes became annoyed when the lorry that had been ordered to convey them to the station was late. As he waited, growing increasingly irritable, they heard a loud explosion followed by smoke rising into the air. The railway station had been sabotaged; the driver and porters were quick to point out that their delay had been an advantage!

Eva and Mary left to take up passages on a troopship from Port Said to Singapore, leaving Bowes to follow by air when the habeas corpus cases pending had been completed. In fact, because of the destruction of Jerusalem's railway station, it was necessary for them to do part of the journey to Port Said by armoured car. The next day Bowes successfully resisted the petitions of 3000 illegal immigrants against their detention. When he returned from court to his office the assistant inspector general of the Palestine police and army security officials were waiting for him with instructions to leave Palestine immediately because an imminent attempt on his life was known to have been planned. So, that afternoon, 22 November 1946, he was escorted to Kalandia airfield outside Jerusalem in a convoy of armoured cars. He flew out in a Puss Moth aeroplane normally reserved for the air officer commanding Palestine – just he, the pilot and room for one suitcase. It had an open cockpit and navigation was by flying to the coast, then turning left and following the coastline along the edge of the Sinai desert. When they spotted Port Said they turned south and followed the Suez Canal towards an RAF airfield near Suez. This reliance on visual navigation was made more hazardous because of a sandstorm. Providentially, with fuel low, a break in the storm occurred just at the right moment to spot the canal and they landed safely as darkness fell. Bowes was met and driven north along the canal to Port Said where he was reunited with Eva and Mary. Thus, the next day all three were able to sail for the Far East on the Royal Mail steamship *Andes*. It saddened them that their departure from Palestine had to be marked by feelings of joy and relief rather than regret. Bowes always made the point that, despite his experiences in Palestine, he was neither anti-Semitic nor pro-Arab but vehemently anti-terrorist.

## Hong Kong: 1947–51

The *Andes* was still in its wartime guise as a troop carrier, but it had originally been a luxury liner that sailed between Britain and South America. Bowes shared a cabin with three army officers as far as Bombay, while Eva and Mary shared theirs with another woman and her two-year-old son. Their initial impressions were not promising because they arrived at the correct doorway to find what looked like the scene of a recent and very violent fight. When left unsupervised to have a rest, the little boy had amused himself by spreading his mother's lipstick, rouge and nail varnish over most of the nearby surfaces and on his sheets. Luckily, he and his mother also disembarked at Bombay, so Bowes was able to join his family for the remainder of the voyage to Singapore.

Three hot and tedious weeks ensued while a search was carried out to find passages to Hong Kong. Raffles Hotel had not been refurbished since the Japanese left at the end of the war and it was dirty and run-down. Friends in the legal department in Singapore were very hospitable; they arranged for the family to be allowed to use the club swimming pool as their guests and invited the travellers to join them on Christmas Day. Just before the end of December berths were found on yet another small and very war-battered cargo ship, which carried a dozen first-class passengers and many lower deck ones. The centre of the

178

ship, including the bridge, was entirely enclosed in steel mesh netting and barriers, a customary precaution in the South China Sea because of the risk of pirates among the lower-deck passengers taking over the ship. On New Year's Eve the captain hosted a small party for the first-class passengers at which, for the first time, the Griffins heard the use of the word 'side' in pidgin English. The ship's cat had disappeared and the captain told us how, on making enquiries, a Chinese crewman had told him that 'Outside makee topside, inside makee chow' – a warm hat and a good meal!

On 2 January 1947, in fine but cold weather, the ship sailed into Hong Kong's magnificent harbour, the wrecks of sunken vessels clearly visible as the pilot steered through them until the correct buoy was reached. A launch came alongside in which the passengers were to be taken ashore and George Strickland, who had been acting as attorney general until Bowes could arrive, was aboard it to meet the family.

The launch took them to Queen's Pier, at that time at the centre of the waterfront of Hong Kong Island and the scene of all formal arrivals and departures. It was not far from the Supreme Court building on the top floor of which Bowes was to work. The Griffins were then driven up the Peak to Magazine Gap, where they were to stay in the house of old friends, the director of public works and his wife, Vic and Thelma Kenniff. The Kenniffs had also been in Jerusalem and Thelma had worked with Eva in the Custodian of Enemy Property office; they were very kind and hospitable. Hong Kong, a bare 16 months after the defeat of Japan, was still an extremely battered and shabby place. Nearly all the houses on the Peak had been wrecked, either by bombing or looting, and on first viewing the house that had been allocated to the attorney general was a mere shell of four walls – with no roof, no floorboards, no doors, no window frames and no stairs. Anything that could be used as fuel had been stolen during the war years. In the high humidity and without a roof the internal walls were green with mould and the garden, including a large area that had once contained two grass tennis courts, was a jungle. It had been used as an anti-aircraft site and it also had several brick-lined caves tunnelled into the hillside beside the drive where ammunition had been stored. The twin house next door, which shared the garden and drive and had been allocated to the commissioner of police, was just as badly damaged. Nothing, however, could detract from their position or from the superb view. Despite the Kenniffs' great kindness, 'the lodgers' were an imposition and it must have been an incentive to him, as director of public works, to ensure that repairs to No. 275 The Peak were given priority!

The general atmosphere in Hong Kong in early 1947 was one of dilapidation. As Bowes described it: masts of sunken ships protruded from the sea in the harbour; buildings all over the island had been bomb damaged and looted; and all the public services – ferries, electricity, water supplies, drains, sewage, trams and telephones – had only been partially restored. All were awaiting spare parts from Britain, which was still also affected by postwar difficulties. Commodities of all kinds, including coal, were in short supply, rationed or non-existent. Through the 'civil affairs unit', the military administration governed the colony during the period between Japan's defeat and the governor, Sir Mark Young, taking office once more in the middle of 1946. He had been there at the time of the island's surrender in 1941, and had been interned in Taiwan under very harsh conditions. He had, however, survived in better physical and mental shape than many others and had a firm determination to begin to rebuild the colony.

The Japanese had forced labourers to build a monument to their victory and a memorial to their dead on a prominent site on the ridge at Magazine Gap. The structure dominated the skyline and the view from the harbour; and it was visible from many other points on the island, as well as from Kowloon. It consisted of an enormous concrete obelisk like a skyscraper and, though plans had been made to cover it, it was unfinished and starkly ugly. The governor was determined to demolish it and thereby efface the memory of the humiliating circumstances of its construction. And he insisted that the demolition should take place as publicly and noticeably as possible. The army's demolition experts advised that the monument should be 'slimmed down' to make the explosion less dangerous, and this was done. Finally, the great day arrived and many people gathered at a safe distance higher up the Peak from the ridge on which it stood to watch its destruction. They included the governor, Eva, Mary and the Kenniffs, whose house was one of those closest to the monstrosity. Bowes remained in the house, however, and opened all the windows as a precaution to protect them from the explosion. He heard a terrific noise and a wave of grit and dust engulfed the house and garden so quickly that Bowes received a cut on his forehead, not having ducked away from the open window fast enough.

It was a morale-boosting symbol of the end of any trace of the Japanese occupation and it was almost as though it sent a signal to revitalize the colony. Suddenly, spare parts for machinery began to arrive, buildings were repaired and repainted, roads were mended and more stock began to appear on shop shelves, especially food from Australia. Both the civil service and commerce hired more staff and new investments poured in. When Sir Mark Young retired as governor later in 1947, he had overseen the start of a remarkable restoration and revival. The new governor, Sir Alexander Grantham, took over a colony that showed every sign of its future prosperity.

The Hong Kong Planning Unit, which guided the interim military administration immediately after the defeat of the

Japanese, had been set up in London while the war was still in progress. George Strickland, now Bowes's immediate deputy as solicitor general, had been the legal officer working with that body and had been in Hong Kong since September 1945. At that stage the military controlled by proclamation and regulation, but now it was a question of restoring normal government.

The Japanese had destroyed all records, books and legal documents, including the entire code of the colony's prewar laws, the so-called Fraser edition – they had also beheaded the unfortunate John Alexander Fraser, who had been an assistant attorney-general of Hong Kong, in October 1943. It had been the usual practice for colonies to exchange complimentary sets of their laws with other colonies for reference purposes. An appeal was sent out via the Colonial Office for any such volumes to be sent to Hong Kong and Bowes felt it was a good omen when a complete set arrived from his own old office in Uganda. Thus, he could use these as the basis for the important work that now faced him and his colleagues in the legal department.

The massive enterprise of redrafting the laws of Hong Kong took Bowes and three colleagues, appointed under the revised edition of the Laws Ordinance 1948, three years to complete. The Legislative Council in 1950 recorded a debate on the motion 'That the Governor order by Proclamation that the Revised Edition of the Laws shall come into force'. The Honourable Leo d'Almada e Castro, KC, paid tribute and said that it was a task 'of magnitude ... which produced so satisfactory a result'. He went on to say that, in accordance with practice in the past, the editions were called after their principal editor.

> This edition, I take it, will be known as 'Griffin's' and, in my submission, a most suitable name because the ease of reference in all of its volumes makes it particularly

suitable for any 'griffin'.[8] This publication has been the result of much time, labour and skill on the part of the Legal Department ... the work is particularly creditable in my opinion because that Department is, as we all know, a very much-overworked one these days. It is therefore in my view fitting that the names of the persons concerned with the preparation should be recorded in Hansard. They are the Hon. J. B. Griffin, The Hon. G. E. Strickland, Mr H. A. de Barros Botello and Mr E. H. Sainsbury.

As attorney general, Bowes was also involved in every aspect of the colony's revival, covering the relevant legal aspects and agreements on the restoration of all services and the government's concessions to the companies that operated the telephones, ferries, trams and electricity. The Labour government in power in Britain urged that all such services should be nationalized, but in Hong Kong efficient private enterprise won the day. Another example of the home government attempting to impose its ideology on Hong Kong was the suggestion that municipal councils should be created. As in other parts of the empire, the governor in Hong Kong acted with an Executive Council and Legislative Council comprised of official and unofficial members. This suggestion was not popular. However, legislation, which was most complex and took a year to draft, was duly prepared and sent to the Colonial Office for scrutiny and approval before being enacted in Hong Kong, despite local reluctance. Months went by and nothing was heard of it. During a visit from Lord Listowel, minister of state at the Colonial Office, the minister arrived late for a meeting of the Executive Council. The discussion was dull

---

8. 'Griffin' is an old-fashioned expression, meaning apprentice or learner/ new boy.

and uninspiring until Listowel asked Bowes, as attorney general, what the position was about the municipal council legislation. He was told that the final draft of the bill had been with the Colonial Office for months. Before the disconcerted minister had time to recover from this reply, the senior Chinese unofficial member, Sir Man Kam Lo, joined in saying, 'I add that, as far as any one of my colleagues in this room is concerned, our hope is that we will never see or hear about the Bill again.' They never did!

Inevitably, there were unpleasant legacies of the Japanese occupation. One was the case against a cadet officer named Kennedy Skipton who had disobeyed orders. At the time of the enemy victory he had offered his services to the victors to continue working on a project he had been heading to increase local food production; in other words he was a willing collaborator and had avoided internment. He was dismissed from the colonial service.

Of course all the normal duties associated with preparing legal advice and prosecutions in criminal cases had to be carried out. The return to prosperity had in fact increased criminal activity, thus illustrating that poverty is not the only cause of crime. Murders, drugs, large-scale thefts, corruption, fraud and Triad protection rackets all brought more work. However, the arrival of three experienced former colleagues from Jerusalem to join Bowes in May 1948, after the end of the Mandate in Palestine, eased the situation in the legal department. This was then reorganized into three sections covering the judicial department (under the chief justice, puisne judges, registrar of the supreme court and magistrates); the legal department (attorney general, solicitor general, crown counsel); and the registrar general's department, with that officer, his assistants who covered the registration of companies, patents, designs and trade marks, land registration and official receiver in bankruptcies.

While Hong Kong began to prosper again, the situation in China worsened. The communists under Mao Tse-tung were challenging the nationalists under Chiang Kai-shek for control of the vast country. As these forces gained more power, the wealthier and more powerful nationalist supporters headed for Hong Kong as refugees. They brought with them all they could carry in gold, jewellery (inserted into their corsets) and huge packing cases of possessions and valuables that they intended to sell to finance their new lives abroad.

In addition to the affluent refugees, there were also hordes of others flooding into Hong Kong by every means – train, junk and sampan. This tidal wave of people overwhelmed all the services in Hong Kong, causing health and fire hazards in the squatter encampments that sprouted up overnight on any vacant patch of land. The police, fire, medical and other departments met this further challenge with great efficiency.

The last remnants of the nationalist government held out in Nanking, the British embassy also moved there and, because of the need to maintain radio links with the embassy, HMS *Amethyst* was sent up the Yangtze River and from the communist-held north bank the ship was fired upon. The captain was killed and there were other casualties. The naval attaché at Nanking, Lieutenant Commander Kerans, was sent aboard from the embassy to take command. Weeks passed while diplomatic representations were made in an attempt to allow the vessel to return to sea, but they all failed.

Fuel and other supplies were in short supply and eventually the ship made a dramatic escape, at first under cover of darkness, past the guns. It so happened that the Griffins that night were dinner guests of Admiral Madden aboard HMS *London* and were present when he was handed the signal announcing that *Amethyst* had rejoined the fleet. They were later among those at the naval dockyard when *Amethyst* arrived, but it happened in such a heavy tropical downpour and poor visibility that it was not until the battered vessel was actually alongside that the shell holes and structural damage could be seen.

The crew had endured many anxious and uncomfortable weeks and volunteers offered to have the men stay in their homes to help them recover from the experience. The Griffins took two guests, a leading stoker and a telegraphist; the former was very talkative about his adventures, the latter very silent. They were welcome and appreciative guests, but it was almost impossible to understand what the talkative one was saying because, in addition to his strong Geordie accent, he had lost his dentures in the Yangtze battle.

The total control of mainland China by the communists presented new dangers and problems to Hong Kong. The colony's defences were strengthened and many new troops arrived, taking up their posts near the border in the New Territories, which Bowes visited with other members of the Executive Council's defence committee.

His earlier experience of drafting emergency regulations during troubled times in Palestine had been useful and these were used to control the squatter encampments set up by the refugees. Their shantytowns were appalling and only hardy Chinese, accustomed to poor living conditions, could have tolerated them. In the interest of health and general sanitation, the sites were compulsorily cleared from time to time, the inhabitants moved to other sites and the accumulated filth and rubbish burnt, thus preventing what could have been serious cholera outbreaks. Much later, the Hong Kong government built whole new housing estates to cope with the enormous population increase.

Many of the richer Chinese had escaped by air and the pilots had simply walked away, leaving their aircraft, which belonged to the nationalist Chinese government, on the runway at Kai Tak with the question of their ownership unresolved. In the small confines of Kai Tak airfield, these 40 to 50 abandoned aircraft were a nuisance. Britain recognized the new communist government, but with America continuing to support the nationalists, the aircraft became prizes over which the two factions argued.

Bowes argued that any party interested in owning the aircraft would have to prove its claim in the Supreme Court of Hong Kong. An assertion had been made that an American company had purchased all the aeroplanes from the nationalist government; and the sudden arrival in Hong Kong of an American group headed by Colonel Bill Donovan, the famous wartime leader of the OSS (the predecessor of the CIA) supported this claim. They attempted to convince the governor, with whom they secured an interview, that the aeroplanes were now American property. The governor referred them to the attorney general. Bowes insisted that the aircraft should remain in Hong Kong and under guard, pending the claim being examined by the Supreme Court. Donovan assured him that he would be reporting to the US government that Hong Kong's attorney general was a communist sympathizer, at which point Bowes told him to leave his office.

This charge was one Donovan repeated to the press at a conference he called the next day. In a leader in the next edition of the *South China Morning Post*, it was reported that 'the Attorney General appears to have seen Donovan off satisfactorily.' Bowes's opinion and advice was based on the fact that, in international law, state property – for example the nationalist government state-owned aircraft – devolved on successor national governments. Further, the constitution of the Chinese state airlines required that any sale of its assets had to be authorized by a majority of the Chinese government's Legislative Yuan, which of course had not been given. The American government's refusal to recognize the new communist government was contrary to international law. In contrast, the British government's acceptance that China was now under communist control also meant an acceptance of that regime having ownership of all government property, including the aircraft.

The Americans put pressure on the British government over the case and Bowes was sent to London for discussions with His Majesty's government, with instructions to bring all records of the case with him.

He was booked to fly with Pan American Airlines and on checking in at Kai Tak airport he brought the package of documents with him as hand luggage. However, he was told that the package was too large to remain with him in the cabin and that it would have to go into the aircraft hold. The flight to London at that time lasted for many hours, with several refuelling stops, and it was further delayed by fog in London. When they eventually landed, a Foreign Office car and official met the plane. A meeting with the foreign secretary was scheduled for that morning, despite Bowes feeling dirty, tired and unshaven from the long journey. His suitcase duly came to light from the hold but there was no sign of the package of papers. He insisted on returning to the tarmac and personally searched the hold of the plane, which was about to take off again for the onward flight to the United States. He was told that the missing luggage must have inadvertently been offloaded at one of the earlier stops and he was assured that it would soon be traced and returned to him.

Deeply concerned and suspicious, he set off in the Foreign Office car in a very annoyed state, exacerbated by a very painful tropical ulcer on his leg. He refused to attend any meeting until the next day and went instead straight to his hotel, hoping that his suspicions were unfounded and that the package's disappearance was an innocent mistake and that it would be found.

After a night's rest, the first meeting of the day was to be at the Colonial Office and, as it happened, it provided some amusement. The Colonial Office minister opened the discussion by saying, 'Well, what about Seretse Khama?' He was told that the meeting was about the case of the Chinese aircraft in Hong Kong and not about the Seretse

Khama marriage controversy, which was then headline news. The minister realized he had come to the wrong meeting and left.

The real meeting followed with the top legal official at the Colonial Office, Sir Kenneth Roberts-Wray, and his opposite number, the Foreign Office legal man, Sir Eric Beckitt. General dismay and suspicion was expressed over the missing documents. Later that day and again on the next, Bowes had meetings with the secretary of state for foreign affairs, then Ernest Bevin, in his magnificent room overlooking St James's Park and the Horse Guards. Ernest Bevin was clearly unwell (he died soon afterwards). He asked no questions but gave Bowes a lecture on the necessity and virtue of recognizing the new Chinese communist government whatever the Americans felt and did. As he put it bluntly, 'Better to keep talking to them boys!' The meetings were short but agreeable and, as the foreign secretary's view was exactly the same as the Hong Kong government's, Bowes felt that his journey had not really been necessary. Further discussions and meetings were held: one with the United Kingdom's attorney general, then Sir Hartley Shawcross, and at the Foreign Office, during which news came via the American embassy that the package had been found in the United States and was being returned. So much for the story of it being inadvertently unloaded at some stop *en route*! This incident did, however, alert officials in London to the devious methods being used by people in America who were determined to maintain their support for the nationalists, such was the hysterical fear of communism at that time.

In 1983 a book was published entitled *The shadow warriors: the OSS and the origins of the CIA*. It described 'Wild Bill' William J. Donovan as 'a gung-ho battle-happy Republican New York lawyer ... a former Assistant Attorney General and one of the two most highly decorated officers in American history'. President Truman had abruptly sacked Donovan from his position as head of the OSS on the grounds that he had grown 'too big for his boots'. It was extraordinary that Donovan, who displayed all the subtlety of a tank, could ever have been an effective leader of the United States secret and security services. Thus, there was general acceptance in London that Bowes's stance with regard to the legal ownership of the aircraft had been correct and he returned to Hong Kong, this time making sure that he flew BOAC and not with an American company.

The threat from the communists was nevertheless a real one and it increased when North Korea was overtaken. The South Koreans wanted to remain non-communist and the resulting war there involved many British troops in the United Nations force, although the main effort came from the Americans via their occupation troops still at that time based in Japan. The support for the British troops came from Hong Kong and involved economic sanctions against the Chinese and some tricky legal decisions, always with the full awareness of Hong Kong's vulnerability.

Despite Bowes's considerable official responsibilities and volume of work, family life in Hong Kong was pleasant. Once repaired, the house – 275 The Peak – must surely have been one of the most desirable four-bedroom houses in the world; it was comfortable and well designed. It shared a hillock named Gough Hill on the Peak with its mirror image, No 276, where the commissioner of police, Duncan MacIntosh, and his wife Kathleen lived. They became close friends as well as totally congenial neighbours and, inevitably, the two houses became known as 'Law and Order'. The view down to Deep Water Bay, Repulse Bay, Shushun Hill and Aberdeen fishing village and out across the sea to the other small islands was stunning, at least on clear days, for during many summer months it could be shrouded in damp mist. At night the twinkling lights from the fishing junks out at sea were spectacularly beautiful.

There had once been two grass tennis courts in the garden, but after the war it was felt that one shared hard court would be enough; and cheerful, friendly tennis and tea parties were held nearly every Sunday. In the first two years the beaches were deserted and swimming was possible. However, once public transport improved, the beaches became too crowded for pleasure and thereafter swimming was an occasional treat in club swimming pools at Sheko and May Road. There were many attractive walks on the Peak along the narrow roads originally constructed by the Victorians; on the whole they were well shaded, with wonderful panoramic views across the harbour and to the hills behind Kowloon. At first these roads were quiet because all the houses were still in ruins. It was an eerie feeling to stand inside the shell of what had once been someone's fine house and to see the sad traces of its former owners – perhaps an empty, rusty tin trunk with a name on the lid, or rotting, torn photographs of people who had been interned and often died during the Japanese occupation. In an amazingly short time nearly all the ruins, like the Griffins' house, had been restored or replaced by fine new ones or large blocks of modern flats.

Our social life in Hong Kong was very busy. Each year the 'national' associations – St George's, St Patrick's, St Andrew's and St David's – organized full dress balls and there were invitations galore to cocktail parties, dinner parties and Chinese meals (which Bowes did his best to avoid). Since total strangers often hosted these functions, it was a matter of some delicacy to decide whether to accept or to have a prior engagement. Many of these pretentious receptions were held in the Hong Kong Hotel where luckily there was a second strategically placed door, enabling one's attendance at an unavoidable function to be limited to shaking hands on arrival, followed by a steady beeline across the room to the exit. 'In and out in seven minutes!' It was always necessary to be wary of any hospitality or gifts that could possibly constitute a bribe. More to the Griffins' taste were gatherings of their own friends on a much less lavish scale and family picnics around the island and the New Territories. They also enjoyed visits to Macau, Lantau and Chungchau by ferry. Hong Kong was such a colourful exotic place, full of interest and diversity, and the five years they spent there were a wonderful experience.

When leave became due once more towards the end of 1951 there was every indication that the job in Hong Kong would continue, but, in accordance with her usual practice on such occasions, Eva nevertheless carefully packed up and listed all their belongings. Her efforts were a sensible precaution. While on leave Bowes was offered and accepted promotion to a chief justiceship and they never returned to Hong Kong. The packing cases were already prepared for shipment to yet another destination, this time to their great joy a return to deeply loved Uganda, the country that always remained their favourite.

## Uganda: 1952–56

After an enjoyable leave in London, Ireland and Guernsey, with a visit also to Scotland, the Griffins left Daphne embarked on her career with Shell, having obtained her degree at London University, and Mary at school in Sussex. They sailed via the east coast to Mombasa and travelled by train up to Kampala, an interesting and spectacular trip that they much enjoyed. On arrival Bowes's younger sister Alice and her husband Arthur Boase, as well as the judges and some judicial department staff met them. The joy of the reunion with his sister and brother-in-law and meeting their children was particularly great; the war and the course of their respective lives had meant they had seen little of each other since 1936, so there was a lot of catching up to do.

A surprising welcome came also from Yusefu Kigongo,

formerly their head boy during their previous existence in Uganda, who was keen to re-enter their service, which of course he did.

Bowes now found himself working in the court building in Kampala that had been constructed when his father, Charles Griffin, had been chief justice 22 years before. The house that had been the official residence then was now used as a rest house for visitors from the rural areas and the modern chief justice's house on Nakasero Hill was unfortunately an architectural disaster, built on several different levels with badly designed rooms. Nevertheless, it became 'home' once the packing cases arrived from Hong Kong.

Eva had a real gift for organization, detail and hospitality. A wide circle of friends and golf for exercise made life pleasant, while their safaris, which were necessary on first arrival to carry out an assessment of judicial staff and buildings away from the capital, gave them a chance to re-explore old haunts. Bowes found the court rooms, offices and houses used by his colleagues shabby and in need of much repair and modernization and set about the matter like the proverbial new broom. The state of the rest houses, where judges on circuit had to stay, also left much to be desired, a situation that also improved rapidly. The then governor, Sir Andrew Cohen, was quick to accept the need for improved standards both in the judicial department and the police stations, and necessary funds were made available.

The major effort, however, was to instigate and supervise the enlargement of the main high court building in Kampala itself, increasing the number of courtrooms and office accommodation. This was well and seamlessly done, following exactly the architectural style of the building constructed during Bowes's father's time.

Crime levels had risen with other more desirable advances since his last session in the colony, but the most interesting case in the four years that followed was that involving the Kabaka (King) of Buganda.

In 1900 an agreement had been made between the then Kabaka of Buganda and Britain; it laid down that Buganda would retain a large degree of self-government within Uganda exercised by the Kabaka, the chiefs and the *Lukiko*. In 1953 the governor, Sir Andrew Cohen, whose socialist leanings were towards the dissolution of the empire and speedy independence for all its territories, began to plan for Uganda's future. For the sake of economic and political viability he wanted a united country with a central legislature whose members would be elected on a constituency basis and on political party lines.

This proposal threatened Buganda's special position and was therefore unacceptable to the Kabaka, who refused to cooperate despite lengthy negotiations. Indeed, the Kabaka pressed for the complete secession of Buganda and its independence from the rest of Uganda. This was at total odds with the idea of a strong, united country.

Under pressure from the governor, Her Majesty's government withdrew recognition from the Kabaka under the terms of the 1900 agreement and sent him into exile in an RAF aircraft to Britain. Regents were appointed to rule Buganda in his place.

The Kabaka and his legal team challenged the governor's action, and Bowes heard the case against the governor and the Uganda government. He ruled that the Kabaka had not acted disloyally in wishing to continue under the terms of the agreement made at the beginning of the century and should not have been exiled.

It was a humiliation for the governor but an example of the independence of the judiciary. The Kabaka was reinstated and his position maintained for a few more years before being affected by the fearful troubles that followed independence. It was an immensely popular ruling and perhaps an indication that many people were content to live with traditional rulers under the colonial yoke and were in no hurry for the imposition of democratic freedom.

However, the whole concept of colonialism was under threat from those with fashionably left-wing views and the movement to reject British rule was unstoppable (and has, some feel, proved regrettable).

In 1954 independence was still some years away and Kampala was a peaceful place in which to live. The city was attractive and well maintained in that the grass was kept cut and anti-malarial measures were taken. It covered seven small hills and the valleys between. The various religious denominations and the Kabaka's palace were prominent landmarks among the red-roofed houses, and the shopping areas had many small Asian-owned shops and a few larger banks and business enterprises. It was hard to believe that so much would soon be changed.

The high point for Bowes in 1955 was the knighthood bestowed on him at an investiture at Buckingham Palace in July that year. His father had also been knighted during his tenure as chief justice of Uganda 30 years earlier and his uncle, Sir Henry Daly Griffin, was similarly honoured for his judicial career in India, making it a 'hat-trick' of knighthoods in one family.

Further health problems made early retirement seem advisable and it was with great sadness that Bowes left Uganda in 1956. He was given a tremendous sendoff, with presentations and speeches from the many organizations with which he had worked. In particular, the Kabaka gave him a farewell reception at his palace, which the governor attended despite the history in the background. The Kabaka led Bowes around the vast crowd gathered for the occasion, all of whom, according to custom, prostrated themselves as the two men approached. As Bowes recalled later, it was difficult to conduct an inspection or show appreciation when everyone concerned was facing downwards!

Once more the family's possessions were crated up and shipped, this time to England and an uncertain future.

## England: 1956–57

The Griffins rented a flat overlooking the common and the cricket pitch on Mount Ephraim in Tunbridge Wells. This was a difficult period for them both as they tried to adjust to a new way of life. They disliked the cold winter and found the incessant round of necessary cooking and chores tedious, although they cheerfully tried to learn and adapt. The enforced rest helped Bowes's recurrent duodenal trouble and he soon felt better and realized that at only 53 he still wanted to work.

For a while a job in the legal department of the Iraq Petroleum Company seemed to be a solution. But he did not enjoy commuting and it was also awkward at his age to break into accepted seniority in the commercial world, among men with years of experience in that field so different from his own background. Fortunately, after a few months an escape back to a life they understood and liked came about. The cases were filled once more, the flat sublet to old friends and the luggage labels for the Union Castle Line *Edinburgh Castle* filled in, as they were to sail to Cape Town.

## Northern Rhodesia: 1957

The new appointment was only to be a temporary one. It so happened that the then chief justice of Northern Rhodesia, Sir Peter Bell, was an old friend and former colleague from Jerusalem days. He was due to go on leave and normally the senior puisne judge would have acted as chief justice. However, the man in question was elderly, due to retire soon and had health problems, so the Colonial Office decided that Bowes should go out and do the job instead. They were to travel by sea to Cape Town, stay there for a week and continue the journey to Lusaka by air. Peter Bell met the Griffins on their arrival and took them to his house, which they were to take over for the next few months. However, within days of his departure on leave, Peter Bell sadly collapsed and died while consulting his doctor in London. The stay in Northern Rhodesia was therefore longer than first anticipated, for they needed to remain until a successor could be found for the territory; in the end the Griffins were there for eight months.

One 'repeat' experience, following on from his work on supervising the extension of the high court in Kampala, was to oversee the new and very fine building under construction in Lusaka; it was next door to the existing one, which was little more than a large bungalow. The work was not very far advanced, but the Queen Mother's visit to Northern Rhodesia was to take place a few months later. Thus, a major effort was made to complete the central entrance front so that she could officially 'open' it during her visit, even though only a shell existed behind the façade! On the great day the Queen Mother duly accepted the scissors Bowes passed to her to cut the ribbon, but she insisted on giving him a coin in return for good luck. The coin was mounted later on a pen tray and kept on his desk.

In 1957 Northern Rhodesia formed part of a federation with Southern Rhodesia and Nyasaland, and each country's judges served on the joint Court of Appeal. This provided an opportunity to visit the other two areas in the course of duty. In the case of Nyasaland the visit was a nostalgic one as well as a reconnaissance. It was nostalgic because it was Bowes's birthplace and his early childhood home, a house called Nyambadwe in Blantyre, was still standing. At that time it was the home of Judge Southworth, another former colleague from Jerusalem who had made a remarkable recovery from the terrible injuries he had suffered in the King David explosion 11 years earlier. It was strange to find the house looking very much the same as it did when Bowes had last seen it in 1910, with the only very important difference being modern plumbing! Later, in the tiny and rather crumbling bungalow that had been his father's office, he sat at the desk immediately beneath a photograph of his father that formed part of a 'rogues' gallery' of former Nyasaland judges hanging in the room.

The other reason why the visit to Nyasaland was of special significance was that Bowes had been offered the position of the first speaker of the newly-planned parliament of Nyasaland, about to be created that year as a preliminary to parliamentary democracy before the country gained its independence. The offer was said to be confidential, so he found it amusing to arrive at the hotel in Blantyre to find a queue of would-be servants waiting to be interviewed if he took the job. In the event, a more attractive offer came, so he never returned to the land of his birth other than on this brief visit as part of a session of the Court of Appeal.

With the exception of the copper mines – at the peak of their prosperity and the source of much of the wealth for all three territories at that time – and the magnificent Victoria Falls on the Zambezi River near Livingstone, Northern Rhodesia seemed a dull country compared with Uganda. Nevertheless, it was a happy few months and they made many good friends there. The arrival of Sir George Paterson, the newly appointed chief justice, meant that the sojourn was over. So, with Mary, who had been doing secretarial work in the African education department in Lusaka, they once more packed up and set off for England, having a memorable holiday in Rome, Florence and Venice *en route* and arriving home in time for Christmas in Tunbridge Wells.

## Uganda: 1958–62

This time the Griffins knew that their spell in England would be brief because Bowes had been appointed as the first speaker of Uganda's new parliament, the National Assembly, and they returned to Kampala with great alacrity early in 1958. It made them happy to be back among familiar friends and places, although this time the job was very different. Establishing parliamentary democracy in Africa was challenging. As the National Assembly building was still under construction, there was yet another project to supervise and it was interesting to adapt all the practices and customs of Westminster to suit Uganda, which involved training the staff as well as the honourable members. Bowes was kitted out with a superb speaker's robe, worn with his own full bottom judicial wig for ceremonial occasions. For everyday use and in the heat, however, he wore a barrister's wig and a loose, light black gown. The most fortunate and happy circumstance of this period was that he had the support of two most congenial and capable colleagues, Philo Pullicino and a man whose surname was Pennington, always known as 'Pen'. In addition, the women who operated the special machines from which Hansard was transcribed were fast (in the sense of work) and efficient.

After a few months in a small modern house on Kololo Hill as a temporary measure, the Speaker's Lodge in Makindye became ready for occupation. It was an attractive, older house that had been redecorated and improved, and servants who had worked for them before once again looked after them. They especially enjoyed its attractive and well-established garden stocked with flowering tropical shrubs. Sadly, this pleasant and interesting existence could not last.

In 1962 Uganda gained its independence, which, far from filling him with joy, Bowes faced with foreboding. He remained as speaker for three months after Independence Day and then resigned to comply with the new constitution, which required that all members of the National Assembly be Uganda citizens. In reply to the many and generous tributes paid to him, Bowes ended his thanks with the wish that honourable members would be strengthened at all times to persevere in their heavy responsibilities to ensure the liberties of peace, prosperity and happiness of all the peoples of Uganda, and thus ensure a fine destiny for Uganda. Inevitably, among other kind gifts, he was presented with a spear and shield, so African traditions as well as parliamentary ones were kept.

## Northern Rhodesia/Zambia: 1962–65

Much to his relief, Bowes was once again able to avoid retirement in England. Following an operation his health was better than it had been for years and he was delighted to be able to accept another contract appointment to return to Northern Rhodesia as chairman of the Public Service Commission.

By this time the end of the colonial era was signalled in Northern Rhodesia too and the commission's task, an urgent and difficult one, was to make every effort to train and promote local Africans to take over running the country when independence came. There had been many years of financial stringency and little secondary education had been available, so the shortage of well-educated and qualified men was serious. An additional complication arose from the dissolution of the federation and the return to local responsibility of matters that had been under federal control from Salisbury. Many European and South African staff had to be replaced, while locally employed people would have to work under new conditions of service.

With a certain sense of grief, for other former colonies were already showing signs of corruption and chaos, in the autumn of 1964 Bowes and Eva attended yet another series of independence celebrations, this time presided over by the Princess Royal. They remained in Lusaka for a few months more, but in 1965 they finally left Africa for good.

## Malta: 1965–92

With memories of how difficult they had found English winters, the Griffins decided this time to settle in Malta.

They bought a plot of land in the centre of the island, not far from Mdina, and had a house built to their own design. This was something that Eva had always wanted to do. She maintained that, having moved so often in the previous 35 years, she had accumulated considerable knowledge of what features to avoid.

The dream house was provided with wonderful storage, fitted cupboards and other details that pleased them both. But while it was being built they realized, as they drove each day from their rented flat in Sliema to inspect progress, that it was in fact not the right solution. It was too far from shops and public transport and would become impossible if they could no longer drive in their old age. So the house was sold without their ever having lived in it and they bought, instead, a large and attractive flat on Tigne Seafront in Sliema, which worked well for them both for the rest of their lives.

They were very contented in Malta. This happiness came especially from their friendship with Philo and Laura Pullicino and a number of other old friends from their previous nomadic existence, and most especially from the loving care and support given to them by Doris Spiteri, her sister Lily and Mary Vella for many years. All was well until about 1973 when Eva's health deteriorated and she died in the wonderfully run Blue Sisters' Hospital where she was so well nursed, on 28 November 1977, just ten days before their golden wedding anniversary. Bowes continued to live in Malta but paid regular visits to his daughters in London and Oxfordshire and to his sisters in Suffolk and Sussex, usually flying over at Easter, in August and at Christmas time.

In old age he frequently commented on how exceptionally fortunate he had been, not only in his family and friends but also in having had a life of such variety, and with work that was truly interesting and to his taste, for all of which he was grateful. However, he was greatly distressed that in so many countries in which he had served much that had been achieved by all those who had been in the colonial service was being destroyed and lost in the post-independence turmoil of local mismanagement and corruption.

In 1984 he remarried to a twice-widowed Scots woman named Margaret Lever. She died in 1991, by which time he was exceedingly frail and his eyesight was deteriorating. Nevertheless, he was determined to stay in Malta and, thanks to Doris Spiteri and nursing support, he was able to do so. Towards the end he said quite clearly that he was weary and used the words 'Nunc Dimittis'. He died early on the morning of 2 February 1992, the Feast of the Presentation when Simeon is recorded in the Gospel as having used just that expression.

# 4

# Mary and John Hannah: the third generation

In 1957 I (Mary Hannah) had just completed my secretarial training when my father, Sir John Bowes Griffin, was asked to go to Northern Rhodesia as acting chief justice.

## Northern Rhodesia/Zambia: 1958–69

I accompanied my parents to Lusaka, but found life a trifle flat after the gaieties of London and the commuter belt. Indeed, social life in Northern Rhodesia seems to have been as formal in the late 1950s as it had been for my aunt Alice in Uganda 30 years earlier. The general relaxation in social attitudes in England during those years, especially in the post-Second World War era, made matters seem worse. Fortunately, I had completed my secretarial training and my parents (unlike Alice's in the 1920s) encouraged me to take a job in the African Education Department. I learnt to drive, played tennis and enjoyed Northern Rhodesia on a short-term basis. On returning to London, however, I knew that I would prefer to remain there rather than go to Uganda, where my father had agreed to become speaker of the legislature; in fact I had no wish whatsoever to live in Africa again. Fate willed otherwise because, within a few days of starting work as 'tea girl and dog's body' in the Northern

Rhodesia office in the Haymarket, I met my future husband, John Hannah, and rapidly changed my mind.

John had served five years in the Sudan political service before joining the colonial service and, arriving in Northern Rhodesia fresh from 'independence' in the Sudan, he was understandably sceptical when a senior official assured him (in 1955) that there was every chance of a full career in Northern Rhodesia. In fact this confident prediction was quite wrong, for the territory became independent barely nine years later.

John had served in four bush stations during his first tour, but for the first few months after our marriage, which took place in Uganda, we lived in Lusaka where he worked in the department of the member for education and social services. We were allocated a small modern house known as a 'PK Special'. PK is the local name for a 'loo' and it was so called because its architectural design afforded a fine view of the PK from the front door!

For a few months in Lusaka, classed in civil service terms as a 'temporary married woman', I worked for the governor while one of his regular secretaries was on leave. This was far too demanding a job for my limited skills and restricted previous experience, but it was exceedingly interesting. It was the time of constitutional negotiations between emergent African politicians, local officials and the Colonial Office. The European politicians' quite different ambitions and the existence of the Federation of Rhodesia and Nyasaland further complicated the process.

Early in 1959 John was transferred to Chinsali in the Northern Province, about 500 miles from Lusaka, as district officer. This was my first taste of a bush station and I tentatively drew up a 'big' shopping list before we left Lusaka. I learnt my first lesson when John told me to increase all quantities considerably.

Living in Chinsali in 1959 was no different from the earlier generations' experiences of colonial life. There were about eight expatriate officials, but only two or three married ones among them. We cooked on Dover wood-burning stoves and the fridge and lamps ran on paraffin. There was little for me to do: clerks at the *boma* did nearly all the office work, though the district commissioner's wife was given the special 'perk' of being allowed to type confidential documents. Fortunately, sewing and gardening proved absorbing and our house rapidly became a halt for many itinerant friends, especially missionary White Fathers for whom we had enormous respect. After a while I learnt a little Cibemba and began to run sewing and knitting classes for some of the African women. This contact of course removed the isolation of being one of the remote Europeans and made life far more interesting and satisfying – at least I was no longer totally idle.

John, by contrast, was working exceedingly hard on many development schemes, and spent weeks on end touring, bicycling on bush paths from village to village. By this time political feelings were more apparent and there had already been an ugly incident in which a district officer had been injured by a spear when on tour accompanied by his wife. For this reason I only went on tour with John once because he was quite determined to avoid the possibility of having to deal with a political incident while being concerned for my safety. Other wives were still touring but he was adamant, so I stayed at home. I was fortunate in being able to pay many happy visits to Shiwa Ngandu, the home of Sir Stewart Gore-Browne and Major and Mrs Harvey. The packed bookshelves in that lovely place were a real treat, for the lack of access to reading matter was the worst deprivation of all, though we did order books and magazines from 'home' regularly.

At this time the practice began of shouting and shaking fists in the *kwacha* (meaning independence, freedom or dawn) gesture as Europeans drove past, which I found very unpleasant. It contributed to the realization I already had, from hearing about the Mau Mau in Kenya and seeing refugees streaming out of the Belgian Congo in 1960, that the expatriate minority would be exceedingly vulnerable unless political aspirations were met speedily. In the two-and-a-half years we were in Chinsali there was a considerable increase in 'incidents' such as chopping down trees to make road blocks, burning beer halls and schools, and driving around in packed lorries shouting slogans. The day we left to go on leave in August 1961, we heard that felled trees blocked two of the three roads leading out of the district. With some apprehension we set off via the remaining route and got through without difficulty. We heard later from missionary friends that UNIP activists had kindly waited until our car was seen to pass by because they did not want to delay our departure. This has always seemed a doubtful compliment but at the time we were very relieved to reach the ship in time.

Seeing frightened and dejected Belgian refugees from the Congo made me pack a case full of favourite wedding presents and silver, which from that time onwards we left in England, keeping little of value in Africa and eventually leaving with only four tea chests besides personal clothing. But that was not until 1969. In the interval, from early 1962 when we got back from leave until November 1963, we were in Livingstone where John was based while working on all resettlement and development matters arising from the construction of the Kariba Dam and the flooding of the Gwembe valley. I do not think the pace of life in Livingstone can have been very different in the 1930s when it ceased to be the country's capital. There was little going on but we enjoyed visiting the Victoria Falls and game parks at weekends. The heat must have made concentration and work difficult for the men. I am ashamed to think how idle I was aside from domestic affairs, apart from one week's work in the typing pool set up for the visit of the Monckton Commission, which was enquiring into the federation and ultimately led to its dissolution. There was an election at which some Europeans, who hoped to bridge the gap between extreme European and African parties, fielded candidates, but it was all a bit half-hearted, for the tide could not be stemmed.

In November 1963 we had just moved to Namwala when we heard of the assassination of President Kennedy. This staggering news was in such stark contrast to the sleepy, timeless atmosphere of Namwala. It was a small station, with few residents and very old-fashioned, cool houses set among well-established jacaranda trees on the banks of the Kafue River – an idyllic spot, with hippos eating the vegetables we tried to grow, and fishing and bird watching on the river. John, as district commissioner, had to organize an election while we were there and I helped to count the votes. Not many returning officers have to wait for the votes to come from the polling stations by canoe and, with the rainy season at its height, much of the district was flooded.

We were sad to leave Namwala but there was a further move in store. We were to go back to Chinsali, by this time a most unhappy district due to the unrest created by the fanatically religious followers of a Bemba woman called Alice Lenshina. In 1953 Lenshina, a baptized member of the Church of Scotland mission at Lubwa, five miles from Chinsali, claimed to have had visions, which some people think may have been brought on by epilepsy or from consuming hallucinogenic mushrooms. At first the Church of Scotland missionaries tried to keep her within their sphere of influence by suggesting they hold shared prayer meetings. However, it gradually became clear that Lenshina and her adherents were becoming a separate Church. It was a time when local politicians – not least Kenneth Kaunda, who also came from Lubwa – were beginning to agitate about an end to colonial rule, and there was some anti-European feeling. A new, wholly African Church thus had great appeal and, as well as heady ideas of independence, Lenshina's claim that she could release her followers from their superstitious dread of witchcraft was attractive. As part of the ceremony for joining what had become known as the Lumpa Church, the converts had to surrender all their amulets and charms to Lenshina or to one of her deacons. Far from a sense of release from fear, however, the dread of magic powers was transferred in her people's minds to Lenshina herself, now thought to have gained control of what previously had been each individual's charms. Although many of her converts had previously been attending the Church of Scotland or the Roman Catholic missions, their Christianity often did not rule out a little clandestine old-fashioned insurance of a primitive superstitious kind, and Lenshina's power grew rapidly for this and other reasons, spreading from Chinsali to neighbouring districts, the Copperbelt, Lusaka, and even to non-Bemba areas like the Southern Province around Livingstone and into Southern Rhodesia.

Lenshina borrowed and adapted ideas and religious practices from established Christian prayers and rituals; lorry loads of Lumpa followers would be heard cheerfully bellowing out many splendidly stirring hymns as they drove around the district in the early years of her movement. Gradually, however, as more and more people changed their religious allegiance, relations with the established churches started to deteriorate. At this point Lenshina refused to obey the traditional chiefs and began to disagree with the political activists. This of course led to frequent disputes and by March 1964, which was when we returned to Chinsali, there had already been some serious clashes, with several murders by Lenshina's followers and the reprisals that followed.

The Lumpa adherents had left their home villages and, without the customary permission from the local chiefs, had built new ones, which they encircled with stockades and ditches. The movement was by now very rich, with headquarters at Sione, about five miles from the district offices at

Chinsali, in the area of Lenshina's home village of Kasomo. A very large brick church had been constructed there, and other Lumpa villages had more modest ones. This evidence of generous financial support must have further annoyed the UNIP activists, for Lenshina and her group refused to bow to their demands or contribute to party funds. When ordered to leave their illegal villages and return to recognized ones, the Lumpa people refused to obey.

Independence was scheduled for October 1964, and possibly it was felt that if the new country of Zambia were to start with a united population under its triumphant politicians, the Lenshina question would have to be settled before the colonial era ended. A major confrontation was inevitable.

An encounter between some policemen and a group of Lumpa followers during a routine patrol sparked off an appalling and most distressing three months. It was in June 1964 and it followed a family dispute between a Lumpa schoolboy and his uncle, a member of UNIP. The boy's supporters attacked the uncle's village, and it was while this was in progress that the police unexpectedly arrived. Some arrests were made, but more Lumpa men appeared and they released the prisoners. Later, on following up the report of the earlier incident, the police officer in charge of Chinsali district, Senior Inspector Leslie Ellis, Detective Inspector Harwood and about a dozen constables went to the village where four Lumpa men armed with spears confronted them. One man threw a spear; their 'war cry' of 'Jericho' was heard and the police officer gave the order to fire. The man who had thrown the spear was shot and killed.

Many more Lumpa, who had been hiding and were also armed, then appeared. The police force was small, and was ordered to withdraw. The only exit from the village was a narrow one, and it involved negotiating the humps and bumps of a patch of ground on which cassava was being grown. Leslie Ellis tripped over a mound and while on the ground he received a spear wound through his arm; thanks to his tough police boots, however, he managed to fight off another man who was attacking his feet with an axe. A constable was also wounded. The police returned to Chinsali and reported to John that there was a rumour going round that the *boma* would be attacked that night. We were, of course, totally unprotected and vulnerable. Fortunately, the night was uneventful.

A mobile police platoon arrived in Chinsali and began to patrol the district. The gravity of the situation was discussed and in Lusaka it was decided that Prime Minister Kenneth Kaunda (who was soon to become president) should attempt to persuade Lenshina and her people to return to their legal villages and mend their ways. Kaunda flew to Chinsali to speak to party officials and to tell them that Lumpa people should be allowed to return to normal life without reprisals of any kind. Lenshina met Kaunda, but only after John had gone to Sione to persuade her to do so. At first he was told that Lenshina was away in the bush collecting medicinal plants; another man said she had gone to the Copperbelt and a third that she was in her house but very ill. John expressed concern and went into the house on the pretext of seeing her to arrange transport to get medical attention. Lenshina was in bed but promptly hopped out, fully clothed and with her shoes on, saying that she had known that the ruse would not work!

Kaunda gave Lenshina an ultimatum, telling her that she had seven days in which to persuade her followers to return to their original villages. She maintained that her people did not want to live among 'beer drinkers and fornicators', and subsequently they made no attempt to obey.

On 22 July a mobile police platoon went to a village called Chapaula in a further attempt to persuade the people to move. They in turn claimed that they would move if they had transport. Two days later when the same unit, led by a young inspector called Derek Smith, returned to Chapaula, they were attacked as they entered the stockaded village and a man who had been hiding behind the gate speared Derek Smith in the back. The police withdrew, pursued by the Lumpa, and the unfortunate European officer collapsed and was repeatedly stabbed until he died. Constable Chansa was also killed. Later I typed the report for the preliminary inquiry into this incident and there were over a hundred stab wounds on Smith's body. Lumpa women and children had inflicted most of these after he had fallen to the ground. Chansa had suffered in a similar manner.

When John received the report of what had happened at Chapaula he immediately arranged for another mobile police platoon to accompany him to the area so that he could recover the two bodies and assess the situation. On arrival there he saw how large and substantial the stockade around the village was. Angry abusive shouts came from the villagers behind it who were clearly in a very belligerent mood, in contrast to the thirty or so African policemen with John who, aware of their colleagues' fate earlier that day, were extremely apprehensive; they could not be relied on and in any case would have been seriously outnumbered. A discreet withdrawal was ordered and, on his return to the *boma*, John contacted the provincial police officer at Kasama by radio and obtained his agreement to have as many armed European police officers as possible sent to Chinsali.

About sixty men arrived the following day, together with the provincial commissioner and senior police officer for the Northern Province. John accompanied the main group to Chapaula, while the provincial commissioner flew overhead in a small aircraft. The plan was that from the air he would be able to assess the situation behind the stockade. A red Verey cartridge would be fired to signal that the villagers were in place and armed, or a green one if all appeared calm. Sadly, the Verey pistol did not work, so a message was tied up in a handkerchief, weighted in some way and dropped from the aircraft. John and his companions saw it fall into a patch of cassava, but it proved impossible to find even though they hunted for it on their hands and knees.

The decision was made to enter the stockade, despite not knowing what the potential resistance there might be. A breach was made with some difficulty, for the structure was crude but strong. The force went a little way into the village, in line abreast, moving forward as far as a prominent anthill onto which John climbed while the others stood still. Through a loudhailer John called out in Cibemba (the local language), urging the Lumpa people to lay down their weapons. While he was doing so one of the policemen, a Mr Jordan, shouted a warning that he could see a man aiming his gun at John, who climbed down hastily before handing over command to the assistant commissioner of police who gave the order to fire. This clash led to the deaths of 35 villagers and the surrender of the remainder.

The women were as aggressive as the men, and it should be said that one of the strongest beliefs of Lenshina's people was that their cause was so righteous that they could come to no harm; no bullet would wound them. Even after that day at Chapaula they tragically continued to hold onto that belief; the 35 deaths had failed to provide the salutary warning that might have saved other lives. Meanwhile, amid rumours and genuine attacks on other non-Lumpa villages, hundreds of very frightened men, women and children sought refuge at the missions, causing acute problems over accommodation, food, hygiene and health.

These horrible incidents convinced John and all the local officials that the situation was beyond civilian control; the police were simply not trained to deal with such encounters. John therefore flew to Lusaka to see the governor and it was decided that the army should intervene. On John's request the governor agreed that whenever soldiers were sent to deal with a settlement, John or one of the district officers who also spoke Cibemba should accompany them, and that they

15. John Hannah, District Commissioner Chinsali, appealing to Sione Lumpas to surrender (*source*: John Hudson, *A Time to Mourn*, 1964).

should always first attempt to persuade the Lumpa people to surrender peacefully. This pattern was subsequently always followed, but without success.

On 27 July, a bridge near the White Fathers' mission at Mulanga was damaged. A police patrol was ambushed when its vehicles had to stop there because of the damage, and Inspector Jordan, who had alerted John to the danger of attack at Chapaula, was killed.

On 29 July, two battalions of the Northern Rhodesia Regiment arrived in the district, as well as three more mobile police platoons. By making Sione the army's first objective, an attempt was to be made to capture Lenshina in the hope that opposition would collapse if she were arrested. On 30 July John accompanied the troops under Lieutenant Colonel Baker's command to Sione. As before at Chapaula, John appealed to the Lumpa to surrender, but before he had finished using his loudhailer a group of men hidden in long grass attacked some of the troops, so firing began. There was initially a nasty moment when it seemed as if some of the African soldiers might turn tail, such was the ferocity of the Lumpas; fortunately, discipline won and they obeyed the yelled commands of the European officers. At intervals the army ceased fire, enabling repeated appeals for surrender to be made, and 436 women and children did so, but sixty-six men and seven women were killed and more than a hundred were wounded. The weapons captured filled a lorry, but Lenshina unfortunately escaped.

While the battle was going on at Sione, we waited anxiously in Chinsali. I happened to go down to the little post office and suddenly a stream of panic-stricken people ran towards me from the township, for a rumour had reached them that Lenshina had broken out of Sione and was coming with her supporters to attack the *boma* area. I have never forgotten the experience of a large crowd of shouting, terrified people suddenly surrounding me, but in view of the circumstances their fear was understandable.

Each Lumpa village was dealt with in turn while the search for Lenshina continued. There was a night-time sortie to some caves at the far end of the district, where she was said to be hiding. It was the coldest time of the year and John set off with the security forces with thermoses of hot drinks, for it was really chilly at 3 a.m. I was of course left behind, 'guarded' by an elderly district messenger armed with an ancient elephant gun, who slept peacefully on the floor in the kitchen while I opened and shut the fridge and stoked the wood stove beside him, to keep the fire going for the men's return. In the end Lenshina slipped out of the district and was detained in next-door Kasama, from where she was taken to spend the rest of her life under restriction in a distant part of the country. Similar events occurred in other neighbouring districts that had also been affected by the Lumpa resistance and civil disobedience. One White

Father from a Catholic mission in Lundazi was killed, and altogether the tragic final total of casualties was huge, amounting to over 700 killed and 400 wounded.

The turmoil was all the more shocking since Northern Rhodesia had historically been a peaceful territory; even the pre-independence political demonstrations had been comparatively mild, compared, for example, with the horror of the Mau Mau in Kenya. We were thus faced with a totally new situation and found it difficult to understand why one group of Africans was attacking another from the same tribe rather than targeting Europeans, which at a time when it was fashionable to be anti-colonial might have been more likely. The damage to villages and people by each side was more tragic given that they were all living at such a pathetically low subsistence level anyway, but great efforts were made to restore calm.

Suddenly, Chinsali was inundated with visiting officials, politicians and missionaries hoping to mediate, and medical teams were sent in to cope with the wounded. Providing them with food and accommodation was difficult because there were only about a dozen houses and a very small rest house with only four beds; and we were 500 miles from the capital and about 140 miles from the nearest small grocery at Kasama. The ground in front of our house filled with vehicles and tents, and the very basic airstrip was much used to bring in supplies. Luckily, my parents were in Lusaka at that stage and my mother organized a mini Berlin Airlift with the help of the supply flights, which made catering for over 300 visitors through our house in four months a lot easier!

The governor, Sir Evelyn Hone, and Kenneth Kaunda were among those who came, and Kaunda, astute politician that he was, deeply impressed our servants when he carried his own dirty plate out to the kitchen to speak to them. In an attempt to help maintain some normality, I had kept the knitting and sewing classes going throughout this whole period. One day we received a visit from Chinsali's strident new member of parliament who arrived with a clutch of henchmen. He said that the classes were an example of 'paternalism' and pushed in front of me to harangue the women, while I *sotto voce* replied that, if anything, they were an example of 'maternalism'! The women listened to him impassively, but never stopped plying their needles and when he eventually left they burst out laughing. They were critical of his position and told me that they definitely wanted the classes to continue, which perhaps suggests that at heart they were neither anti-colonial nor particularly interested in politics.

By the time order had returned to the district John was due to go on leave, so we were in England on Zambia's Independence Day in October 1964. We returned to a completely different setting – Chingola on the Copperbelt. In contrast to bush station Chinsali this was suburbia in Africa, with many South African expatriates working on the copper mines and a large, previously exclusively European township. John was now called the district secretary, the colonial term 'commissioner' having been discarded, and this was only one of the many changes to which he and the other former British officials had to adjust. The unilateral declaration of independence in Rhodesia meant petrol rationing in Zambia, and suddenly it seemed a good idea to conform by getting an identity card.

Many of our friends had left at independence and in both Chingola and subsequently Lusaka – where we ended our African saga – we had an odd and rather lonely existence, maintaining a low profile so as not to tread on anyone's toes. In place of the former officials and their wives with whom we had been familiar, most of the other Europeans around were now from a strange new breed; they were the diplomats representing the many countries anxious to establish links with newly independent Zambia. Fortunately, the births of our two children kept boredom at bay, but my experiences in the hospital and the visible lowering of standards in such things as law and order, postal, water and electricity services all combined to make our return to England welcome. When it came in June 1969, I was sad to say goodbye to friends who remained, but delighted that our new life would be safely out of a continent that seemed to be beset by political and economic chaos.

## Turks and Caicos Islands: 1971–73

An unexpected postscript to our colonial life came from 1971 to 1973 when John went on contract to the Turks and Caicos Islands in the West Indies. Those two years were an endurance test. After Africa's wide expanses, an island seven miles long by one mile wide felt claustrophobic, and the place offered little except heat, sand, wild donkeys, water shortages and monotony. It was discouraging to be in a territory in which poor communications, a shortage of funds, inadequate rainfall, infertile soil and tropical inertia combined to stifle any attempts at development. It was a relief finally to settle in England and we have thus been fortunate in avoiding the long separations from our children because of their schooling that those serving overseas formerly had to face.

There were many other families like ours in which successive generations served the crown abroad. As an old man Charles Griffin was heard to exclaim, half in anger, that since his decision to join the colonial legal service in 1901 none of his descendants had lived settled lives. Whether our nomadic existence was genetic or contagious, three generations have had experiences of great interest and variety. Inevitably, there are sad memories, but thankfully many more pleasant ones. The men of the family contributed greatly to the law, peace, health and development of the territories in which they served, and those of us who were mere dependants of officials were privileged to share a way of life that is now a part of history.

# References

Boase, Alice, *We Reach the Promised Land*, available from M & E Publishing, 32 Awatea Road, St Ives Chase, NSW Australia 2075, email <knowlden1@bigpond.com>

Garland, Vera with L. G. Stratton, *Ryalls: A Woman and Her Hotel*, Blantyre: Society of Malawi

Lamport Stokes, Barbara, *Blantyre: Glimpses of the Early Days*, privately published by The Society of Malawi, PO Box 125, Blantyre, Malawi

# Index